# INSTRUCTOR'S MANUAL

SIXTH EDITION

# Prentice-Hall

# Handbook for Writers

**DONALD C. RIGG**

*Chairman, English Dept.*
*Broward Junior College*

**Glenn Leggett**

*Grinnell College*


**C. David Mead**

*Michigan State University*


**William Charvat**

*Late of Ohio State University*

ISBN: 0-13-695700-5

Printed in the United States of America

# INTRODUCTION

The Instructor's Manual for the sixth edition of the
Prentice-Hall Handbook for Writers has been revised to provide answers for exercises in that edition. In addition to
sample exercise answers, it contains suggestions and comments which hopefully will be of assistance to instructors
in relationship to various parts of the text. Since no
two instructors ever teach a course in exactly the same
way, the various possible approaches which will be presented
will undoubtedly vary greatly in their appeal to individual
instructors. In this connection, three basic assumptions
have been made. The first is that a manual for a handbook of
this type can provide assistance to busy instructors, who
often lack the time to work out appropriate exercise solutions. The second is that most instructors are constantly on the alert for new ways of handling assignments;
as a result, comments can suggest means for varying class
routines and can provide ideas which will inspire in-
structor-derived approaches. The third is that inex-
perienced instructors can benefit from a somewhat detailed
manual, since guidelines or suggestions are generally
appreciated by those who are teaching a formal course for
the first time.

The Handbook provides a considerable number and
variety of exercises and suggested writing assignments.
It is hoped that this arrangement will serve the needs of
instructors who have students of widely divergent backgrounds and abilities. There should be enough material
to facilitate intensive application in particular areas
of student weakness; at the same time, many similar type
exercises vary in degree of difficulty. The versatility
of assignments which is consequently possible should
provide a means of assistance to weaker students and at the
same time provide more challenging work for students with
better backgrounds.

Since composition, as much perhaps as any other
subject, is an area wherein a great deal of subjective
judgment must always be exercised, it would be presumptuous
to pretend that this manual has all the best answers. The
suggested exercise answers and comments are consequently
offered in the spirit of helpfulness and suggestion and are
never intended in any way to supersede individual instructor

judgment. Oftentimes, alternative answers may be provided which are just as good as, or perhaps even better than, those listed. In the last analysis, the purpose of the Manual will have been largely achieved if it has been able to provide some good answers and to suggest some effective means by which some other answers can be achieved.

## THE USE OF THE TEXT

A handbook may be used in several ways. First of all, it may be used exclusively as a reference source. In such an instance, the instructor refers the student to the text to study designated areas in which he has demonstrated weaknesses in his writing. Or the student himself may refer to the text for assistance in particular writing phases which may be giving him trouble. Using a handbook in this manner certainly provides one very worthwhile justification for such a text.

A second way in which the Handbook may be used is as a combination reference source and supplementary source for class work in specific areas upon which the instructor desires to concentrate. When it is used in this way, a more comprehensive utilization of the text results, and the text can become the basis for intensive class exploration of subject areas through assignment of explanatory material and exercises and discussions based on such phases. Such a procedure also provides a basis for testing and the generating of written assignments.

A third way in which the Handbook may be used is as the primary curriculum material for the course. In such an instance, extensive use is made of the text and the apparatus which it provides. The resulting course structuring will be one wherein great attention is devoted to student work on fundamentals, an approach that may have particular merit where students are particularly deficient in basics.

A fourth way in which the Handbook may be used is in addition to a rhetoric or reader in instances where the instructor wishes to emphasize training in fundamentals during the first part of the course. In such an instance, the instructor may desire to utilize the Handbook almost exclusively for awhile, then shift to the rhetoric or reader, continuing to use the Handbook as a supplementary text on an as-needed basis or for reference purposes.

## THE ARRANGEMENT OF THE TEXT

The Prentice-Hall Handbook for Writers presents its
material in a generative manner, proceeding in general from
the more basic elements of composition to the larger elements. After a brief presentation concerning the history
of the English language, a section then follows which concerns itself with basic grammar. The next section concerns
itself with basic sentence faults, and this section is
followed by sections on manuscript mechanics and punctuation. The larger elements of the whole composition and the
paragraph are then discussed. Following this, the concern
is with more sophisticated elements of sentence structure,
logic, and diction. Additional sections involve the
library and the research paper, writing summaries, and an
index to grammatical terms.

The above arrangement of materials is obviously not the
only way in which material could have been presented, nor is
it necessarily the best. Many instructors, for example,
will prefer to begin with the section on the whole composition and then refer to additional sections as their classes
continue their composition writing. Others may prefer to
work with the paragraph first instead of the sentence. In
this respect, the text is so structured that the various
sections are more or less independent of one another.
Consequently, the instructor may use the text as he sees
fit, with no concern for the order in which the sections
occur and without any problem of continuity.

The section on the research paper is placed toward the
end of the text since most freshman composition courses
are arranged so that the research paper becomes an item of
concentration in the second term. This fact of course
need not necessarily preclude some use of the research paper
section in the first term if it is desired to include training in documentation during that term.


## UTILIZATION OF THE SECTION KEY

The Prentice-Hall Handbook for Writers provides an
index section key inside the back cover of the text. This
key provides a convenient method whereby the instructor may
refer a student to a particular section in the text.
References to specific areas are indicated by section numbers. This arrangement makes it easy for the student to
locate desired sections, since sections are arranged in

numerical-alphabetical sequence with most such sections being indicated by large numbers at the top of text pages.
Convenient abbreviations are also provided which indicate
many of the principal aspects with which an instructor may
want to concern himself in annotating compositions.  An
example of one way in which the index key may be used is
presented in the preface to the Handbook.  It is suggested
that the instructor spend a little time in familiarizing
himself with the section key, since a thorough knowledge as
to how and where the various aspects concerned are indicated
will save considerable time at composition grading time when
he wants to refer a student to a particular section.


## GLOSSARY OF USAGE AND AN INDEX TO GRAMMATICAL TERMS

The Glossary of Usage and an Index to Grammatical Terms
are sections of the text that instructors may or may not
wish to utilize for classroom assignments.  However, it
should be noted that both of these sections are arranged
alphabetically and as such can be readily referred to by
the instructor and the student.  Similarly, the instructor
can readily refer the student to these sections by directing
him to the term and section involved (Example = "See could
of, 43.").  The obvious implication here is that these
sections can be used most profitably if the instructor has
at least generally familiarized himself in advance with
their contents.  Where this has been done, students can,
in many instances, be quickly referred to definitions that
may assist them to understand some grammatical term or to
enable them to utilize more appropriate diction.

SECTIONS 1-5

BASIC GRAMMAR

Grammar is an ugly word to many students. Their attitudes toward the subject may have been influenced as the
result of two entirely different backgrounds. Some may have
studied grammar only in elementary or junior high school and
may remember it only in terms of tortured pedantically presented drills which had little or no apparent relevancy to
reality. Others may have been influenced by teachers who
may have taken the position that thorough grounding in
grammar is not necessary in order to achieve good writing,
and so chose to spend as little time on it as possible.

Since the emphasis in the Prentice-Hall Handbook for
Writers is basically on composition, no brief is held for
the teaching of grammar as an end in itself. On the other
hand, even though a good grammarian may not be a good
writer--and there are obviously other aspects involved in
good writing than grammar--there can be little doubt that
writing which is otherwise good can be greatly marred by the
use of poor grammar. Certainly, a thorough comprehension as
to the functions words and word combinations play in sentence syntax and the ability to employ tenses and moods
properly will in itself not result in overall good writing.
Nevertheless, such an understanding should result in increased versatility and precision of expression, and writing
which is otherwise good but deficient in these respects is
assuredly not as good writing as it should be.

The use that can be made of sections 1-5 will quite
obviously depend on class proficiency in the aspects which
are involved. With more sophisticated students, it may not
be necessary to use the sections on other than a reference
basis. Weaker students, on the other hand, may profit very
greatly from the discussion and exercises concerning basic
sentence structure.

Many instructors may want to utilize the "Basic
Grammar" Review Exercise at the end of these sections as a
test to determine the level of class proficiency in the
areas covered. Utilization of the exercise for this purpose
can provide a very effective means of ascertaining student

weaknesses. Where weaknesses occur, additional assignments and additional exercises can be assigned to increase proficiency in aspects which require particular attention.

# SECTION 1

## SENTENCE SENSE

A good craftsman knows his tools. He must because he depends upon them for a livelihood. How effectively he utilizes them involves his manipulative skills as an artisan; the more he knows about their construction, their parts, and how these parts work together, the better able he is to understand and to make use of the various capabilities of what he is working with. Much of the same thing is true of the writer, a craftsman in his own right. In his case, the tools are words; the better he understands words, the better able he is to make words work for him and to manipulate them within different types of structures to obtain various rhetorical effects, the better writer he is likely to be. Like other craftsmen, the better he understands the structures of the various devices he has to work with, the better will be his chances of achieving the most effective results as he uses those devices. Since the sentence is one of the basic structural devices a writer will work with, a good understanding of how it works is absolutely essential. To achieve this understanding, knowledge of parts of speech, verbals, phrases, and clauses is necessary.

Section 1a emphasizes the basic sentence patterns: S V, S V O, and S V C. The emphasis here is primarily upon functioning of sentence elements rather than upon parts of speech as such. Prior to the assignment of exercise 1a, instructors may want to stress that the subject as such is more than just a noun--that the subject of the sentence is the part of the sentence that the verb provides action concerning or that the verb provides the means of telling about. Sometimes a subject can take up practically all of a short sentence.

<u>Doing exercises and maintaining regular hours</u> helps one's health.

<u>That he has been working too hard</u> is evident.

In section 1b, which deals with parts of speech, the elements which give most students trouble are perhaps verbals and adjectives and adverbs. For this reason, it may be desirable to do what is possible to insure that students

7

understand the functions of the three types of verbals: the infinitives, the participles, and the gerunds. In particular, students should be made to understand that none of these, even though they are based upon verb stems, look like verbs, and, as a matter of fact, in some instances, are written the same way as progressive verb forms, can never fulfill the functions of verbs in sentences. The above can hardly be overemphasized since the mistaking of verbals for verbs is one of the biggest reasons for students' writing sentence fragments.

Confusion of adverbs and adjectives is a frequent source of student error. Therefore, it may prove to be highly profitable at this point to emphasize that only adverbs can modify adjectives. Such emphasis may help students to avoid future expressions such as <u>most all men</u> and <u>real good manners</u>. Contexts involving the linking verbs used in a <u>seem</u> or <u>appear</u> sense also cause difficulty. For that reason, this might be a good time to emphasize the special function of the linking verb which is essentially to act as an equal sign and to provide the means of saying, from an adjectival point of view, something about a subject. That this is not too well understood by students seems evident from the fact that many, in an attempt to be correct, will say <u>He feels badly</u> instead of <u>He feels bad</u> in commenting upon the health of an individual. Apparently they fail to realize that a predicate adjective, not an adverb, is warranted because of the linking verb.

Section 1d involves a discussion of phrases and clauses, an area which is of importance, since most instructors would agree that students should have a thorough understanding of main and subordinate elements of a sentence; the ability to subordinate properly often assists in achieving greater emphasis and variety in sentences, and, hence in compositional structure. In the recognition of phrases, a construction which it may be desirable to emphasize is one which begins with a participle such as in the sentence <u>Turning to face his opponent, he slipped and fell</u>. An understanding that such words as <u>turning</u> in this type of context are participles, not verbs, may help to assist student understanding of the differences between participles and verbs and may prevent his writing sentence fragments.

One of the ways in which a study of grammar can best heighten an awareness of sentence sense is by requiring students to indicate not only what a construction is but what the purpose of that construction is. Exercises 1d (1) and ld (3) are particularly good in this respect, since they require the student not only to identify by type of clause the subordinate clauses in sentences but to indicate the functions that those clauses perform. Placing emphasis on what constructions do for a sentence would seem greatly to deepen an understanding of how a sentence works; the labelling of a construction as a particular type of clause in such a context serves primarily only as a means toward that end--the way it should be.

### Exercise 1a

Instructors may desire to limit identification of subjects and verbs to main clauses. For the convenience of those who do not, however, subjects and verbs of subordinate clauses are also indicated. Sentence patterns are indicated after each sentence in the order in which sentence patterns occur.

1. The buzzards circled slowly.    Pattern 1

2. War is a disease.    Pattern 5

3. The marchers hoisted their signs and fell into line.    Patterns 2, 1

4. A recent study proves again the dangers of cigarette smoking.    Pattern 2

5. Poverty deprives many children of the education which is rightfully theirs.    Patterns 2, 5

6. Television and radio bring us a great deal of knowledge about current events.    Pattern 4

7. A dictionary, to be useful, must be used.    Passive Sentence

8. We have seen several assaults on poverty through the years, but we have not yet conquered it. Pattern 2

             V   IO           DO

9.  His friends gave Sam a grand reception when he

       V

   returned from Vietnam.   Patterns 4, 1

              V       IO        DO

10.  Local citizens sent the police large numbers of
complaints about increasing burglaries in the
neighborhood.   Pattern 4

## Exercise 1b

    Instructors will vary in the degree to which they
wish to follow traditional classification of parts of
speech versus the classification of recent grammars.
In the following answers, traditional terminology has
been followed quite strictly.  Since the text, together
with the glossary, provides basic information on
inflectional endings and the like, instructors who
follow more recent work classifications will wish to
make some changes in the answers suggested.  All
instructors may find it useful to invite attention to
some terms (e.g. expletive, article, demonstration
adjective) which appear in the glossary or at subsequent
points in the text.


   art.    noun    verb  adv prep art    noun
1.  The  blizzard  raged  out  of  the  Northeast.


   art    noun  prep adv    adj      noun    verb
2.  The  streets  of  most  seaside  resorts  are

     adv       adj   prep  noun
  strangely  desolate  in  winter.


   art    noun    prep noun conj noun    verb
3.  The  pollution  of  air  and  water  continues

    adv      conj      noun     verb conj pron
  unabated  although  scientists  warn  that  it

    verb    art    noun    prep noun
  threatens  the  survival  of  man.

```
              pron
    interj aux v    verb   adj     noun    adv
4.  Stop!  I've  heard  that  joke  before.


    prep adj   art    noun      noun    verb prep
5.  Of  all  the  mistakes  students  make  on

         noun          gerund       noun    verb art   adv
    examinations,  misreading  directions  is  the  most

      adj
    common.


         noun        noun    conj noun  verb  art   adv
6.  Newspapers,  magazines  and  books  are  the  most

       adj      noun     prep      noun
    powerful  weapons  against  ignorance.


    art noun  verb    adv    verb  adj  adj   noun   conj
7.  A  man  should  never  wear  his  best  suit  when

    pron verb  adv    inf     prep  noun   conj  noun
    he  goes  out  to  fight  for  freedom  and  truth.


       noun     verb   conj art  noun verb prep art  noun
8.  Einstein  said  that  a  man  has  at  the  most

     adj   noun conj  noun noun  prep adj     noun
    only  one  or  two  ideas  in  his  lifetime.


    pron verb  adj        adj     inf     art   noun
9.  It  is  sometimes  difficult  to draw  the  line

      prep      noun      conj    noun         adv
    between  "literature"  and  "pornography";  even

     adj      noun      verb   adj    noun
    legal  definitions  reflect  that  difficulty.
```

```
         pron verb    adj          inf        prep     adj
10.   It   is  impossible  to experiment  with  psychedelic

      noun      adj      conj     adj     noun
      drugs  cautiously, because  true   caution

         verb        adj    noun   adv
      would preclude  their  use  entirely.
```

Exercise 1c

1. Organizing a budget, personal or national, requires
   careful planning.

2. Gaining approval from her group was more important
   to Jane than showing loyalty to a principle.

3. Language is the highest and most amazing
   achievement of the human mind.

4. Watching football on TV is the favorite sport of
   millions of Americans.

5. Having worked late into the night, John went to bed.

6. Suddenly the tornado hit the town, ripping roofs
   away from houses, wrenching trees from the ground.

7. Even little girls dream of becoming astronauts.

8. She became interested in social work through her
   summer job in a camp for underprivileged children.

9. For many years the gap between rich and poor in
   South America has been gradually widening.

10. Rising in a graceful arc, the spaceship swung
    into orbit around the earth.

CASE

Case is not something that ordinarily will have to be emphasized a great deal, since case is not nearly as important an aspect of the English language as it is of other languages. There are some types of troublesome constructions involving case, however, that instructors may desire to stress. The possessive case of the personal pronoun, it, for example, is very frequently misspelled as "it's" instead of "its." Therefore, as case is discussed, it might be desirable to draw attention to this fact in the hope of avoiding in the future at least one common spelling error.

Two constructions which are particularly troublesome and which, for that reason, should be specifically discussed are those involving a pronoun that is the subject of a clause which functions as the object of a verb or preposition, and a noun or pronoun preceding a gerund. In this connection, sentences of the type, Who do you think is right? are frequently written incorrectly as Whom do you think is right? and sentences of the type I know nothing of his being there are frequently written incorrectly as I know nothing of him being there.

Two types of constructions in which informal expressions seem very close to acceptance at the formal level are those discussed in sections 2b and 2c. Here, instructors will probably want to exercise independent judgment and decide for themselves whether expressions such as "I thought it was him" will be acceptable in lieu of "I thought it was "he." They may also want to accept expressions such as "It is me" instead of "It is I." Technically, only the latter expressions above are acceptable in formal writing. In actual practice, however, more and more of the informal usages above seem to be creeping into what is generally regarded as formal writing.

Exercise 2

Exercises 2 through 5 deal with problems in which formal and informal usage frequently differ. Answers suggested follow conservative usage. Some instructors, of course, will want to allow more informal choices. Where dictionaries record alternative verb forms, both have been cited.

1. Burgess was the candidate <u>whom</u> all educated people voted for. (relative pronoun <u>whom</u> is object of preposition <u>for</u>).

2. I will consider <u>whoever</u> applies for the position, regardless of creed or color. (<u>whoever</u> is subject of verb <u>applies</u> in subordinate clause <u>whoever applies for the position</u>).

3. It was <u>she</u> who was elected to the student council. (nominative case of personal pronoun, <u>she</u>, is required after linking verb <u>was</u>).

4. Let's you and <u>me</u> get engaged, sweetheart. (<u>me</u> is in apposition with the contracted <u>us</u>, which is the object of the verb <u>let</u>).

5. When we heard the doorbell, we knew it was <u>he</u>. (nominative case of personal pronoun, <u>he</u>, is required after linking verb <u>was</u>).

6. The teacher reported Dick as well as <u>me</u> for cheating. (<u>me</u> is object of verb <u>reported</u>).

7. I appreciate soul music without <u>his</u> telling me what to listen for. (The possessive form of the adjective is required when it modifies a gerund).

8. We discovered Mark and <u>her</u> in the swimming pool. (<u>Her</u> is the object of the verb <u>discovered</u>).

9. Sometimes I think everybody knows more than <u>I</u>. (The pronoun <u>I</u> is the subject of the understood verb <u>know</u>).

10. They considered the logical candidate to be <u>me</u>. (<u>Me</u> is the object of the infinitive <u>to be</u>).

## SECTION 3

### TENSE AND MOOD

Many students have a rather imperfect knowledge of
tenses, particularly where perfect and progressive tense
forms are necessary.  At the college level, it would seem
particularly important, in order to achieve precision of
expression, that the ability be developed to express actions
accurately with respect to time.  How to distinguish between
events happening at different times in the future is a
matter of considerable mystification to many students.  How
to refer to an action completed in the far past as compared
to an action completed in the immediate past also often
poses difficulties.  How to express an action that is more
remotely in the future than some other future action (e.g.,
Tomorrow at noon I shall have been working four hours) can
additionally be a matter of difficulty.  The formation of
passive voice can also be an ability initially beyond the
capability of some students.  The construction of the past
participle is seemingly a very simple operation; yet, many
students have a great deal of trouble in this respect.

For the above reasons many instructors may want to work
with the paradigm for the verb "drag" which is given on page
40 of the text, or with a paradigm for another verb.
Through the use of such a paradigm, participle formation and
construction of passive voice can be studied and differences
in times can be brought out through the employment of
various tenses.  A few of the many possible examples of
tense use which can be brought out by studying the paradigm
are as follows:

### ACTIVE VOICE

PRESENT:   "I drag a sled" means I perform this type of
           action regularly although I may not be doing it
           now.  By comparison, "I am dragging a sled"
           means I am presently engaged in such a process.

PAST:      "Yesterday at 11:00 a.m. I dragged a sled"
           means either that I dragged a sled at that
           particular time or I was in the business of
           dragging sleds, although I may or may not have
           been performing that specific action at that
           time.  By comparison, if I want to indicate that
           at a certain time I was dragging a sled, I would

probably say: "Yesterday at 11:00 a.m. I <u>was dragging</u> a sled."

FUTURE: "Tomorrow at 11:00 a.m. I <u>shall</u> <u>drag</u> a sled" means that I will start the action at that time. "Tomorrow at 11:00 a.m. I <u>shall</u> be <u>dragging</u> a sled" means, by comparison, that I will have already started the action as of the time indicated.

If, on the other hand, I want to speak of an action I have completed after the present but less remotely in the future than a specified time, I can say "Tomorrow at 11:00 a.m., I <u>shall</u> <u>have</u> <u>dragged</u> a sled," whereas if I want to deal with an action that has started and is still continuing at a future time, I can say "Tomorrow at 11:00 a.m. I <u>shall</u> <u>have</u> <u>been</u> <u>dragging</u> a sled."

PAST PERFECT VS. PRESENT PERFECT "Yesterday at 11:00 a.m., I <u>had</u> <u>dragged</u> a sled" means that with respect to a past time prior to another past time, I had taken such an action. By comparison, "I <u>have</u> <u>dragged</u> a sled" means that sometime in the past with respect to the present time, I have taken such an action. Such an expression may also imply that such past action is one that is continuing up to the present, although an even stronger way of indicating such a continuing action would be to say "I <u>have</u> <u>been</u> <u>dragging</u> a sled."

Insofar as mood is concerned, most student difficulties will probably be with respect to the subjunctive mood. This is another area in which some informal expressions are on the verge of respectability, and it will frequently be a matter of judgment as to whether such expressions discussed in the text as "The elm tree looks as if it was dying" will be acceptable in student compositions in lieu of "The elm tree looks as if it were dying." By the same token, one sees more and more such expressions as "I wish that I was taller" in good writing. As a result the instructor will have to decide for himself the degree of formality he will require in his students' compositions.

16

# Exercise 3a-d

1. The protesters <u>lay</u> in front of the Pentagon for days.
   (<u>lay</u> is past tense of verb <u>lie</u>).

2. The Kennedy family <u>used</u> to live in Boston.  (<u>used</u>
   is past tense of verb <u>use</u>).

3. The first man to set foot on the moon <u>became</u> quite
   famous.  (<u>became</u> is past tense of verb <u>become</u>).

4. He was <u>prejudiced</u> against farm life since he had
   <u>lived</u> all his earlier life in the city.  (past
   participles of verbs <u>prejudice</u> and <u>live</u> are required
   to form past passive and past perfect tenses).

5. Plans for the space launch were <u>begun</u> in the spring.
   (<u>begun</u> is the past participle of verb <u>begin</u>).

6. How are students <u>supposed</u> to learn when teachers can't
   teach?  (<u>Supposed</u> is the past participle of verb
   <u>suppose</u>; it is used here in conjunction with the
   auxiliary verb <u>are</u> to form passive voice of verb --
   a construction that gives a great number of students
   trouble).

7. After the government declared amnesty, hundreds of
   political prisoners <u>came</u> rushing out of jail.  (<u>came</u>
   is past tense of verb <u>come</u>).

8. The spy denied that he had <u>stolen</u> the microfilm.
   (past participle of verb <u>steal</u> is required in
   conjunction with appropriate form of auxiliary verb
   <u>have</u> to form past perfect tense).

9. My new bikini <u>shrunk</u>, <u>shrank</u> when it was washed.
   (<u>Webster's</u> <u>New</u> <u>World</u> <u>Dictionary</u> <u>of</u> <u>the</u> <u>American</u>
   <u>Language</u> gives both <u>shrunk</u> and <u>shrank</u> as acceptable
   for past tense of verb <u>shrink</u>).

10. Even Republicans were moved when Lyndon Johnson <u>bid</u>,
    <u>bade</u> the nation farewell.  (<u>The</u> <u>New</u> <u>World</u> <u>Dictionary</u>
    gives both <u>bid</u> and <u>bade</u> as acceptable past tense
    forms of the verb <u>bid</u>).

1. The revolution might have succeeded, if the people had been ready to fight.

2. World peace will be assured when the leaders of all nations sit down and talk to one another. (Set is hardly acceptable here, even in informal language).

3. Any woman would love her husband even more if he were a millionaire. (Sentence expresses a condition contrary to fact; hence, subjunctive mood is required).

4. The Arabs and the Israelis have not spoken to one another for years.

5. After the cars collided, the injured were lying all over the highway. (were laying might be acceptable in informal English).

6. The Titanic, which was considered unsinkable, sank in a matter of hours. (Sunk would probably be acceptable in informal English).

7. He could not swim very well, but he dove beautifully. (Either dived or dove would be acceptable in formal or informal English).

8. She rose from her seat in a rage. (It is doubtful that raised would be acceptable in most informal situations).

9. I will not invite them again because they drank a whole case of beer at my last party. (Webster's New World Dictionary regards drunk in the past tense as archaic; however, drunk as it is used in the above sentence would still probably be acceptable in many colloquial situations).

10. Roosevelt led the nation through some very difficult times. (Lead would hardly be acceptable in the context in even the most informal of situations).

# SECTION 4

## ADJECTIVES AND ADVERBS

Adjectives and adverbs have already been discussed under section 1, sentence sense, primarily as they were involved with respect to linking verbs. A knowledge of parts of speech should help considerably to overcome weaknesses in this area, since basically all the student has to remember to distinguish between the use of adjectives and adverbs is that the adverb is used to describe the manner of the action of the verb and to modify another adjective or adverb. On the other hand, the adjective can modify only a noun or a pronoun.

The comparative and superlative forms of adjectives and adverbs sometimes cause difficulty because of students' tendencies to use the superlative instead of the comparative form when comparing only two as in Ruth was the most beautiful of the two. Certain words (such as good, bad, and delicious) which are compared in an irregular manner also cause some confusion. A good recommendation in this connection is that students refer to a good desk dictionary when in doubt, making sure that they understand that the dictionary lists comparative and superlative forms only when they are listed in an irregular manner.

## Exercise 4

1. The President appears on television almost every week. (Most is an adjective; it requires an adverb, almost, to modify adjective every).

2. Student leaders should take their obligations more seriously. (It takes the adverb seriously rather than the adjective serious to modify the verb take).

3. I felt very bad about having missed him. (Felt is a linking verb; an adjective rather than an adverb is required after it.)

4. The accident was not nearly as bad as it would have been if he had not been driving slowly. (Adverb

19

<u>nearly</u> in conjunction with <u>as</u> modifies adjective <u>bad</u>; adverb <u>slowly</u> modifies verb <u>had been driving</u>).

5. At first even the critics didn't understand <u>Lolita</u> because it's a unique book. (If something is <u>unique</u>, that is the ultimate in that respect; at the formal level, degrees of uniqueness are not possible).

6. The South Pole is the <u>colder</u> of the two Poles. (Only two are being compared; hence, comparative degree is required).

7. Our society is based on the belief that all men are created <u>equal</u>. (The emphasis here is on the status of equality, not on the process of being created; hence, the adjective <u>equal</u> is preferable to the adverb equally.)

8. It is Shakespeare, I believe, who said that a rose by any other name would smell as <u>sweet</u>. (The linking verb <u>smell</u> requires the adjective <u>sweet</u>; the emphasis is on the effect the rose produces, not upon how it itself performs the action of smelling).

9. The lecture was poor because the teacher didn't feel <u>well</u>. (Feel as it is used here is a linking verb; hence, the adjective <u>well</u> is required).

10. John is the <u>tallest</u> of all three brothers. (Superlative degree of comparison is involved; hence, <u>tallest</u> should be used instead of <u>taller</u> which involves only the comparative degree).

## SECTION 5

## DIAGRAMING GRAMMATICAL RELATIONS

Although diagraming is not as extensively employed as
it once was, a section is included for instructors who like
to utilize diagraming as an instructional device. Included
in the text is a number of examples and exercises which
cover most of the basic structural situations that most
instructors will want to deal with. Diagraming is perhaps
particularly helpful in helping students understand that
noun clauses, gerund phrases, and infinitive phrases can act
as complements, subjects, and objects in sentences. Diagraming can also assist in achieving an understanding of the
differences between prepositional phrases and infinitives
and in illustrating the function of the participial phrase,
the misunderstanding of which can frequently lead to the
construction of sentence fragments.

### Exercise 5 (1)

1. Life | is | short

2. Russia | invaded | Czechoslovakia

3. Marijuana | offered | escape
   \them

4. floodwaters | overflowed | riverbanks
   The rising the

5. regulations | irritated | students

### Exercise 5 (2)

1. Balancing the national budget is a gerund phrase used
   as a subject and should go on stilts above the base
   line.

2. With questions is a prepositional phrase modifying
   besieged. It should go beneath the base line.

21

3. To marry well and (to) retire soon are infinitive phrases which should be placed on stilts above the base line.

4. Hunting for antiques is a gerund complement which includes the modifying prepositional phrase for antiques. Hence, the construction goes on stilts above the base line.

5. To ignore others' misery is an infinitive phrase used as a subject; to aggravate it is an infinitive phrase used as a complement. Both should go above the base line on stilts.

## Exercise 5 (3)

1. That it has little power is the complement of the verb is and should be placed above the base line.

2. Toward which both communism and capitalism are moving modifies economy and should be placed below the base line.

3. That their demands were nonnegotiable is the object of the verb insisted and should be placed above the base line.

4. The sentence is compound, having two main clauses: The continent of Africa is now divided into nations on one base line should be separated from tribal divisions are more faithfully observed on another base line by a step line on which but is underlined.

5. That violence is not a viable alternative is a complement and should be placed above the line.

## "Basic Grammar" Review Exercise

### (Sections 1 through 5)

1. Our hopes for Vietnam peace sank when massive bombing of the North began. Sank, not sunk, is past tense of verb sink.

2. The morale of the Arab nations fell very low after the 1967 Six-Day War with Israel. Low is an adjective; consequently, the adverb very, not the adjective real, must be used to modify it.

3. After that war ended, the belligerents all began making plans for the next one. Past tense of verb **begin**, which is **began**, must be used to keep tense consistent with **ended**.

4. **Who** do you think suffered most when the New York City schoolteachers went on strike? **Who** should be used instead of **whom**, because nominative case must be employed for the subject of the verb **suffered**.

5. Before the month ended, he **finished** his term paper. Since action is with respect to past, past tense of verb **finish** is required.

6. International relations may improve significantly if China and The United States **establish** diplomatic relations. Subjunctive mood of verb **establish** is used to express condition contrary to fact.

7. NASA was **surely** delighted when the space shot proceeded on schedule. (**Surely** should be used instead of **sure**, since the word chosen must be an adverb to modify the adjective **delighted**).

8. **Since** the moon **has become** an object of scientific exploration, it's hard to think of it in the romantic terms we **used** to. (**Since** establishes a better time and cause-effect relationship than does when. **Used** is the past tense of verb **use**).

9. Federal law **forbids states'** imposing a poll tax. The sense of the sentence is probably with respect to the present time; hence, present tense of verb **forbid** is required. Also, possessive form of modifier must be used before a gerund.

10. It would **have been interesting** to watch a debate between William Buckley and Stokely Carmichael. Present infinitive is correct after verb in perfect tense. Another correct version of sentence would be as follows: It would be interesting **to watch** a debate between William Buckley and Stokely Carmichael. In latter revision sense of future time is better brought out by use of present infinitive.

11. If Judy **were** coming home tomorrow, I would not leave today. Subjunctive mood is required because a condition contrary to fact is involved.

12. Most students are annoyed by those <u>kinds</u> of teachers who fail to make their courses relevant. <u>Those</u> is a plural and requires a plural noun to modify.

13. Cleveland was the first major American city that <u>had</u> a black mayor. The tense of the verb <u>have</u> must be consistent with that of the verb <u>was</u>; hence, <u>had</u> is required.

14. Many policemen feel <u>bad</u> over newspaper accounts of police brutality. The linking verb <u>feel</u> requires an adjective to express the state of emotion prevailing.

15. The U.S. could only protest the East <u>Germans</u>' building the Berlin Wall. The protest is directly with respect to the action itself, not about it. Possessive form of modifier must be used before a gerund.

## BASIC SENTENCE FAULTS

Sections 6-14 move into an area that gives some students a great deal of trouble. It is an important area,
too, in that errors of basic sentence structure in a composition often impart an air of near illiteracy to writing.
At a more sophisticated level of writing many students, in
the attempt to achieve smooth thought flow between sentences
and paragraphs, will experience difficulty with coherence.
Coherence is also deeply involved on an even more fundamental basis in sentence structure. Poorly written sentences
are even more fatal to the achievement of coherence than the
failure to establish sentence relationships; if individual
sentences are good, the reader has at least a fighting
chance to impose upon them an integration of meaning. If he
has trouble in even getting through the sentences themselves, then the reading task becomes a near impossible one.

## SECTION 6

## SENTENCE FRAGMENT

Students write sentence fragments because they either fail to include a verb (sometimes a subject also is left out) or they fail to realize that certain constructions are subordinate and must have a related main clause before the constructions become sentences. The failure to include verbs often occurs because the student mistakes a participle in a construction for a verb as in His reason for not going being his sore leg. Being, a participle, in the previous construction looks like a verb but isn't one. If trouble is being experienced in the area, it might be worth the time to elaborate a little upon the difference between the progressive form of the verb be, being, and the participle being. If students can be made to understand the difference in function between the participle and progressive forms of verbs, a great deal may be accomplished in the avoidance of sentence fragments.

If some time has been spent on section 1d, "Recognizing Clauses," students should be able to identify subordinate clauses and should not write a subordinate construction as a sentence. If trouble should persist in this area, Exercise 6, which requires the combining of subordinate elements with independent elements, should help. Another approach which might help at this time would be to discuss the various subordinating conjunctions (when, if, as, since, because, etc.), stressing the fact that where these words head a clause, a subordinate clause is involved and, hence, an independent clause must also be present before there is a sentence.

## Exercise 6

Many other variations are of course possible when revising these sentences. In particular, some instructors may desire to emphasize noun clauses by placing subordinate clauses first in the first sentence revisions.

1. The Soviet delegate's walking out of the meeting was his way of avoiding the issue.

26

The Soviet delegate walked out of the meeting.
This was his way of avoiding the issue.

2.  Though he had promised to cut it, Nixon's first
    national budget was the largest in history.

    Nixon's first national budget was the largest in
    history, although he had promised to cut it.

3.  Violence is becoming a tool of political dissent
    chiefly because non-violence can so easily be ig-
    nored by the country as a whole.

    Non-violence can be easily ignored by the country
    as a whole.  Such disregard is the reason that
    violence is becoming a tool of political dissent.

4.  Many doctors refuse to prescribe birth control
    pills because some women have had serious side
    effects after using them.

    Some women have had serious side effects after
    using birth control pills.  For this reason, many
    doctors refuse to prescribe them.

5.  The Beatles decided to stop giving concerts just as
    they were at the peak of their fame.

    The Beatles decided to stop giving concerts.  Their
    decision was made just as they were at the peak of
    their fame.

6.  Soul music was gaining popularity, but many people
    still didn't know what it was.

    Soul music was gaining popularity.  This was true
    even though many people still didn't know what it
    was.

7.  The climax of many new films is the nude scene,
    even when it adds nothing at all to the particular
    story.

    The climax of many new films is the nude scene.
    Such scenes occur even when they add nothing at all
    to the particular story.

8.  The two candidates have identical platforms, the

only difference being in their parties.

The two candidates have identical platforms. The only difference is in their parties.

9. The cortege at President Kennedy's funeral was a long one with rich and poor and young and old all marching side by side.

President Kennedy's funeral was a long one. Rich and poor, young and old, all marched side by side in the cortege.

10. Many young people are considering social work as a career not for the money, but for the sense of satisfaction it provides.

Many young people are considering social work as a career. They consider it not for the money, but for the sense of satisfaction it provides.

## COMMA SPLICE AND RUN—TOGETHER OR FUSED SENTENCE

At the time that the run-together sentence is being considered, it is also a good time to try to achieve a good understanding of the semicolon. One principal purpose of the semicolon is to separate independent elements; an understanding of this fact may assist the student to resist the temptation to provide commas instead of semicolons in the sentence. A rather interesting situation can now also occur if the student has achieved a knowledge of the subordinating conjunctions such as <u>after</u>, <u>when</u>, and <u>because</u>. He may now find that the same conjunctions which may have misled him to write sentence fragments may now be used to form subordinate clauses to avoid run-on sentences and comma splices.

### Exercise 7

In this exercise, two sample answers are given. One involves the use of the semicolon; the other involves subordinating part of the exercise. Several other ways of re-writing the sentences are, of course, possible. In many instances, for example, a colon or dash could be employed instead of a semicolon. Also in some instances separating the original sentence into two sentences would be permissible.

1.  The U.S.S.R. and Red China were technically allies; however, they have been having quite a few problems lately.

    Although the U.S.S.R. and Red China are technically allies, they have been having quite a few problems lately.

2.  General Eisenhower wrote a book about his World War II experiences; he called it <u>Crusade in Europe</u>.

    General Eisenhower wrote a book, <u>Crusade in Europe</u>, about his World War II experiences.

3.  Throughout the 1960's when civil rights bills were being passed, Senator Fulbright was considered a

liberal; in spite of this, he always voted against them.

In spite of Senator Fulbright's being considered a liberal, throughout the 1960's when civil rights bills were being passed, he always voted against them.

4. The North Koreans allowed the crew of the Pueblo to return home; they kept the ship.

Although the North Koreans allowed the crew of the Pueblo to return home, they kept the ship.

5. Most of Hemingway's novels have similar subjects; love and war are two of the most frequent.

Most of Hemingway's novels have similar themes, two of which, love and war, are among the most frequent.

6. The best way to publicize a movie is to say it's "For Adults Only"; then teen-agers will flock to see it.

The best way to publicize a movie to be sure teen-agers will flock to see it is to say it's "For Adults Only."

7. The pollution of water resources is proceeding rapidly; the next generation of Americans may be drinking rationed water.

Because the pollution of water resources is proceeding rapidly, the next generation of Americans may be drinking rationed water.

8. The black students decided they wanted a dormitory reserved to their use; some white students called it "reverse segregation."

Because the black students decided they wanted a dormitory reserved to their use, some white students called it "reverse segregation."

9. It's confusing to try to remember all the organizations called by their initials; CIA, CIO, and USIS are just a few.

It's confusing to try to remember all the organizations

called by their initials, of which CIA, CIO, and USIS are just a few.

10. Some students question whether literature is relevant to them; they should really be asking whether they are relevant to literature.

Although some students question whether literature is relevant to them, they should really be asking whether they are relevant to literature.

## FAULTY AGREEMENT AND FAULTY REFERENCE OF PRONOUNS

Faulty agreement is the type of error which is made by everyone, even though he knows better. The greatest trouble in this area usually involves the vague and indefinite use of the pronouns <u>this</u>, <u>that</u>, <u>which</u>, <u>they</u>, <u>you</u>, and <u>it</u>. For this reason many instructors may particularly wish to emphasize sections 9a-e. Direct assignment of exercises in this area may be advisable in many instances, and even where it is not student familiarization would seem to be in order because of the rather frequent subsequent references that may have to be made to these subsections because of vagueness in compositions.

### Exercise 8a

1. Each of the Congressmen has a special purpose for making this inspection tour. Subject <u>each</u> requires singular form of verb.

2. Either the President or the members of his cabinet were ill-advised about the distribution of farm subsidies. Subject is plural and hence requires plural form of verb. <u>Was</u> instead of <u>were</u> would be acceptable in informal English.

3. Among my favorite books is <u>Nine Stories</u> by J.D. Salinger. Subject of sentence <u>Nine Stories</u>, a book, requires a singluar verb.

4. There are a good many reasons for the tensions between Arabs and Israelis. Plural form of verb is required to agree with plural subject <u>reasons</u>.

5. The burden of sales taxes falls on the shoulders of the consumer. Subject, <u>burden</u>, requires singular form of verb.

6. The crux of the urban problem is overcrowding and unemployment. <u>Crux</u>, the subject of sentence, is singular and requires singular form of verb.

7. The farmer, and not the city dweller, feels down-
hearted when agricultural prices fall. Positive
subject of sentence _farmer_ requires singular form
of verb _feel_.

8. Ten dollars is more than a poor family can afford to
pay for a pair of shoes. _Ten dollars_ is a collective
noun and requires singular form of verb.

9. The main complaint of most college students is the
required courses forced upon them. Subject, _complaint_,
requires singular form of verb.

10. Sentence is correct as it is originally written. In
informal writing _has_ would be acceptable.

## Exercise 8b

1. Everyone should exercise his right to vote.

2. The citizens' group submitted its report to the mayor.

3. Neither of the world leaders was willing to compromise
on his demands.

4. Everybody has his own solution to the race problem.

5. None of the students in the psychology class could
analyze his own dreams.

6. If either a black man or a white man were qualified,
he would get the job.

7. No teen-ager appreciates his parents' sacrifices for
him until later in life.

8. If a physician or a lawyer came to this town, he
would make a good living.

9. Every American citizen should have the right to live
wherever he can afford to live.

10. The Kennedy family has carried on in spite of its
tragedies.

## Exercise 8c

1. Adam Clayton Powell is one of that kind of politi-

cian (those kinds of politicians) who is (are) usually described as "flamboyant."

2. Congress should pass a law that everyone must vote or he will be fined.

3. The committee on admission of new members does not approve the nomination of Mr. Smith.

4. The President with his cabinet members is touring South America.

5. Sentence is correct as it is originally written.

6. Two solutions to national traffic problems have been offered but neither has been tried.

7. Sentence is correct as it is originally written.

8. Sentence is correct as it is originally written.

9. The college president told the militant students he would not put up with this sort of tactics.

10. After thirty, one loses both the rebelliousness and the inventiveness of his earlier years.

11. A chorus of jeers and catcalls was the response to the Vice-President's appearance.

12. Although everyone wants the right to vote, one doesn't always exercise that right at election time.

13. If world peace is to be assured, either the Eastern bloc or the Western bloc must alter its position.

14. The Democratic party lost several of its congressional seats in the last election.

15. If people want to "do their thing," they should be allowed to.


## Exercise 9a

Most of the items in the exercises from this point through section 14 require revision. Clearly, there is no "right" answer to such items. As in previous similar exercises, suggested revisions are merely representative. It is naturally important that the student recognize the various ways in which grammatically incorrect, awkward, or obscure sentences may be approached. Ideally, of course, the student will begin to recognize that his choice of a particular revision in an actual theme will depend upon the larger context (e.g. emphasis, transition). In many of these exercises the instructor may profitably ask the student either to suggest more than one way of revising particular sentences or to defend his choice of a particular revision with reference to a larger context.

1. The record broke when he dropped it on the phonograph arm./ When he dropped the record, it broke the phonograph arm.

2. If Hitler had behaved differently with Stalin, the latter might not have had to take the action he did./ Hitler might not have had to take the action he did had he behaved differently with Stalin.

3. When President Nixon met with Chairman Mao, Nixon felt a new chapter in history had begun.

4. Sidney gave his brother a copy of Catcher in the Rye, which was one of his brother's favorite books. / Sidney's favorite book was Catcher in the Rye, a copy of which he gave his brother.

5. The American people have had a number of inadequate presidents, but Congress has kept such presidents from ruining the country.

6. Marilyn should never have married Jim, she told Susan./ Marilyn told Susan that the latter should never have married Jim.

7. George had a dog which was always scratching fleas./ The dog with fleas, which he was always scratching, belonged to George.

8. Joan told (advised) her friend to take speech lessons.

9. John Steinbeck should have written a biography of Martin Luther King after King won the Nobel prize./

After John Steinbeck won the Nobel Prize, he should have written a biography of Martin Luther King.

10. Kathy was very angry when she visited her mother./ Kathy's mother was very angry when Kathy visited her.

## Exercise 9b

1. The school belongs to the community. It could be the meeting place for all community activities. Students and their parents should work closely with faculty and administrators in developing programs of instruction and recreation.

2. The delegates arrived in twos and threes for the emergency session at the U.N. They stopped only to pose for the press photographers at the entrance. Interested spectators were also streaming in.

3. The crowd watched and moaned and groaned as the computer projected the election returns all across the nation. It was an unexpected defeat.

4. He argued that artists, writers, and even office workers find it necessary to use marijuana as a means of relaxation.

5. He and his opponent made promises to the people of the nation to augment and revitalize the various poverty programs. But such promises were soon forgotten after the election.

## Exercise 9c

1. The poor support of the Third World Program frustrated many students.

2. Martin Luther King's dedication to nonviolence influenced him to become a minister.

3. On election day, people should always vote as an indication of their desire to have a good government.

4. Marlon Brando mumbles his lines and scratches his nose; these tendencies he developed at the Actor's Studio.

5. The government's paying farmers not to grow crops does not help to solve the problem of hunger among poor people.

6. Minimum wage laws should be extended immediately to provide protection for the migrant farm worker.

7. The proposal by the campus paper that the administration provide birth control pills upset school officials very much.

8. The Arabs and Israelis' being constantly poised on the edge of war adds much to international tension.

9. On the far side of the museum is a part which is open to the public.

10. Her real friends weren't bothered because she was self-conscious about her money.

## Exercise 9d

1. She learned to be a meticulous housekeeper when she was a child. / She is a meticulous housekeeper because she learned to keep house when she was a child.

2. He took the shutters off the window frames and painted the shutters (the frames).

3. Because Lucy had never worked a potter's wheel, she supposed working one was easy.

4. Dad admitted to Ross that he stayed up watching television too late. / Dad scolded (berated, admonished) Ross for staying too late and watching television.

5. We called the police station near the church when we saw broken windows in the basement of the church.

6. Because of the frost that had settled over Florida, the orange trees were covered with cloths and fanned by the warmth of smudge pots.

7. After hearing a lecture on underwater sound experi-

mentation, Mr. Eldon had great admiration for the scientists (the frogmen, the engineers).

8. Shirley seems annoyed whenever she meets Rose. / Whenever Shirley meets Rose, the latter seems annoyed.

9. Take the baby out and throw away the bathwater.

10. We plucked off the feathers before we roasted the chickens.


## Exercise 9e

1. Every society expects that some people will not be able to provide for themselves.

2. In Central America one hears of revolutions every few months.

3. The Vietnam Agreement said that all American POW's would be released.

4. Throughout the development of the West, the settlers drove back the Indians and took their land.

5. People of the Victorian era never talked about sex in public.

6. In response to my call, the CIA said it didn't have any openings for summer jobs.

7. The textbooks say almost nothing about our real treatment of Chicanos and other minorities.

8. The government pays out money everywhere except where money is needed.

9. Every generation has a "generation gap."

10. The first few verses of the Bible describe the creation of the world.

## SHIFTS IN POINT OF VIEW AND MIXED CONSTRUCTIONS

Shifts of person, number, tense, and mood are errors that students frequently make in their writing. Many instructors may desire to emphasize subsection 10d on mixed constructions because this particular phase of writing vitally affects the matter of effective transition, a skill that more students probably have difficulty in mastering than any other writing skill.

### Exercise 10a

1. After we heard the lecture, we asked questions.

2. First, carefully clean the surface;  then put the glue on./ First, the surface should be carefully cleaned;  then the glue should be put on.

3. He marked the distance from the crosswalk to the curb, and then he painted a heavy yellow line across the area.

4. David was a fine archer, but he was not strong enough to pull that heavy bow.

5. Mr. Jones put putty around all the window panes, and then he repaired the broken window sashes.

6. After the children dug a path through the snow, they began coasting on their sleds.

7. South Africa has the most plentiful supply of gold in the world, while Mexico leads in silver mining.

8. If you wash it in your dishwasher, highly fired china will last longer.

9. After the campers built the hot fire, they dried their wet clothing.

10. A man needs more than intelligence to be a good legislator; he also has to be a student of human nature.

1. No matter what political party one belongs to, he should listen to all candidates.

2. All people should install safety belts in their cars because safety belts help to save lives.

3. Public opinion polls are based on a cross section of the population but they have occasionally been wrong.

4. When one is feeling tired, a candy bar will give him some quick energy.

5. Leonard Bernstein once said that the New York Philharmonic was second to none.

6. Everyone should have access to birth control information, if his religious convictions permit.

7. The average black American today feels it is less important to imitate white people than for him to develop a feeling of racial pride in himself.

8. Most people enjoy a novel by Tolstoy because its characters are so interesting.

9. If one is dissatisfied with the way the government is being run, he should write to his congressman more often.

10. I tried cigarette-smoking, but it made my throat sore. / I tried cigarette-smoking, but I developed a sore throat.

### Exercise 10c

1. When I smoked cigarettes, they didn't do me any good.

2. First you should learn about the issues, and then you should vote for a candidate. / First, learn about the issues; then, vote for a candidate.

3. *Great* *Expectations* is exciting to read, but Miss Haversham is totally unrealistic.

4. You may prefer to travel by plane, but if the weather is bad, you may have to go by bus.

5. Since I have explained to the professor why I didn't do the work, I expect him to pass me.

6. The Sunday drivers were out in full force, and suddenly there was an accident.

7. I shall be delighted to attend if my husband may accompany me.

8. The university is attempting to revise its curriculum, and the students have been asked to submit suggestions.

9. The library has an intricate system of ordering books, but I might find what you want.

10. The store manager decided to offer free samples, and suddenly the store was packed with customers.

Exercise 10d

1. Since it is a center for the performing arts, most young actors and actresses yearn to go to New York.

2. I tried to explain the generation gap to my parents, whose attitude was such that one would think they hadn't read anything in years.

3. Every effort the student made to explain the problem to his instructor got the student (the instructor) more confused.

4. Allowing black Americans to develop and enforce their unique culture will increase their sense of racial pride and identity.

5. Wage increases are regular; but because of the way the cost of living is rising, they don't make much difference.

6. If sex education is introduced into the elementary school, young people could approach marriage with understanding and with some assurance that marriages would last longer.

7. LSD might be a useful drug, but it is used by young people in such a way that it seems to do more harm than good.

8. The instructor provided much help to his students when he tried a second time to explain the idea.

9. The law requires one to go to high school until of a certain age; besides, the accepted policy is that everyone go through at least high school.

10. If families sat down to talk together, they could avoid many family problems altogether.

# SECTIONS 11-12

## MISPLACED PARTS AND DANGLING CONSTRUCTIONS

Misplaced parts and dangling constructions are aspects that can often promote a great deal of classroom hilarity, since errors in this respect are often of a rather ridiculous nature. For this reason, a little discussion and a few exercises will generally accomplish a great deal because the effects of errors are so often demonstrably ludicrous and hence produce a lasting impression on students. Subsection 11a concerns itself with adverbs such as <u>almost</u>, <u>hardly</u>, and <u>only</u>. Proper utilization of such adverbs frequently gives students trouble. A good illustrative sentence which brings out very poignantly the differences in meaning which are achieved according to the placement of the word <u>only</u> is the following:

    She told Jane to prepare dinner.

Introduction of <u>only</u> into the sentence at various places within the sentence results in the following distinct differences in meaning.

    Only she told Jane to prepare dinner.
    She only told Jane to prepare dinner.
    She told only Jane to prepare dinner.
    She told Jane only to prepare dinner.
    She told Jane to prepare only dinner.
    She told Jane to prepare dinner only.

## Exercise 11a

1. He seemed almost amused.

2. The <u>U.S.S. Constitution</u> docked here just last week.

3. The prisoner confessed only when the victim confronted him.

4. Nearly everyone suffers when unemployment rises.

5. Since she had never appeared on a stage before, she was nearly faint from fright.

6. She refused our offer of help merely because she wanted to be independent.

7. Football is sometimes a violent sport and some players are even badly hurt.

8. The earthquake victims badly needed nurses to bandage their wounds.

9. Reports will be mailed only after all the final examinations are finished.

10. The Administration provided scarcely any funds for poverty programs.


## Exercise 11b

1. In a quivering voice, Susan reported the accident.

2. A small boy in a cowboy suit was found lost on Central Street.

3. The President announced at his press conference last week that he would confer with his cabinet.

4. With admiring eyes, the audience watched the go-go dancers.

5. After three years' attendance, on Friday he dropped out of school.

6. The furnace exploded with a loud crash after the patrons left the theater.

7. The government, without doing anything, is watching the cost of living spiral upwards.

8. For several years, the astronauts looked forward to landing on the moon.

9. After he was nearly drowned, the boy was rescued by a lifeguard.

10. He stopped the car on the street before the house with the green shutters.

1. From a dealer he bought a sports car that had been completely overhauled and repainted.

2. On the TV we watched the quiz program that our college team won.

3. On her hair she uses hair coloring which she buys wholesale.

4. At Times Square, I took a bus that was going uptown.

5. From a neighbor, he bought a Great Dane that was already housebroken.

6. After he graduated from college, he secured with the government a job which lasted twenty years.

7. For her children, she was knitting socks that were warm.

8. For her husband she bought an alarm clock that was guaranteed for life.

9. The new house with three bedrooms was next to the park.

10. He tried with a new approach to get to know the girls.

## Exercise 11d

1. The pilot was told to be prepared constantly for emergencies./The pilot was told to be prepared for emergencies constantly.

2. After the election, the President said taxes would be cut./ The President said taxes would be cut after the election.

3. The story he was slowly reading put his daughter to sleep./ The story he was reading put his daughter slowly to sleep.

4. The motorcycle he was happily riding skidded off the road.

5. The person who in nine cases out of ten succeeds is intelligent./ The person who succeeds is in nine cases out of ten intelligent.

6. The instructor told his students they could ask their questions when the class was over.

7. The passengers were told the plane would take off when it was noon./ When it was noon, the passengers were told the plane would take off.

8. Without doubt, religious faith is a comfort to many people./ Religious faith that knows no doubt is a comfort to many people.

9. The men who were beating on the wall began shooting wildly./ The men who were beating wildly on the wall began shooting.

10. I promised I would tell her all about it when the movie was over.

## Exercise 11e

1. The President promised, if the budget permits, to consider instituting a wage-supplement law.

2. The owner of the discotheque asked the boys to produce proof immediately of their age.

3. The availability of birth control information helps to reduce effectively the number of unwanted children.

4. The student body voted to abolish fraternities from campus for once and for all.

5. Black Americans are determined never again to settle for subordinate status.

6. The president of the university tried to intervene tactfully and quietly between students and police.

7. The problem in Vietnam is to resolve successfully the differences between North and South.

8. The major nations of the world regularly decide to reduce their armaments complex one day in the near future.

9. It's helpful to send in your tax return immediately after the first of the year.

10. You have to accept willingly the idea that you are your brother's keeper, or the condition of man will never improve.

## Exercise 11f

1. After years of smoking heavily, she made an effort to stop.

2. From the top of the stairs, he handed her the box.

3. Because they are not protected by minimum-wage laws, migrant workers are underpaid.

4. After answering several questions, the President announced the plan to recognize Red China.

5. If you ever see a drunken driver, you should immediately contact the police.

6. Despite strong objections from her parents, Peggy is going to study music and painting.

7. Although they did not succeed, the Soviets tried to establish a missile base in Cuba.

8. Albert Schweitzer lived and worked for many years in a primitive hospital in the jungles of Africa.

9. During the party, the uninvited guest slipped in the door that was nearest the garden.

10. After his long illness had kept him confined so long, the Senator's hope was to return to Washington.

## Exercise 12a

1. To one visiting New York for the first time, the sky scrapers were truly impressive.

2. Since its members knew little about Asian customs, the first presidential tour was not entirely successful.

47

3. Paris reveals its eternal variety to one sitting at an outdoor cafe.

4. The police arrested the derelict who was lying on the sidewalk.

5. Since the tabletop was made of glass, I handled it carefully.

6. While I was driving at top speed, the road took an unexpected turn to the left.

7. I realized that the Verrazano Bridge, which spans the Narrows, was one of the longest in the world.

8. Since the animals are fearless and uncaged, visitors to game preserves must be careful not to excite them.

9. The airport delays were endless while we waited for the fog to lift.

10. Since he was a foreigner, his ingnorance of local customs made him feel helpless.


## Exercise 12b

1. After he got up in the morning, he began the day with a good breakfast.

2. When she received word of her husband's return, her eyes filled with tears.

3. When the car was inspected, a large dent was found in the fender.

4. Because he read constantly, the doctor was forced to prescribe glasses for him.

5. After the suspect had been released, new evidence was submitted to the police.

6. When he opened the closet door, the boxes on the shelf tumbled down.

7. Before he transferred to the new school, his mother took him in to meet his future classmates.

8. When one rides in an airplane, the landscape acquires a new beauty.

9. When I checked the answer sheet, my errors became clear to me.

10. As they prepared the launch, they examined the space ship several times.

## Exercise 12c

1. To plan a college program, one must keep career goals in mind.

2. To become a concert pianist, one must spend many years in study.

3. If one is to be a good citizen, he must have some knowledge of government procedure.

4. To eliminate malnutrition, they issued foodstamps to the poor.

5. In order that the record can be appreciated properly, the volume on the record player should be high.

6. To find out why the wheel shakes, one must drive the car over fifty miles an hour.

7. If one is to be completely immune to polio, several innoculations may be necessary.

8. If it is to be a financial success, a minimum of one hundred performances of a play is necessary.

9. One needs a neat appearance to impress a prospective employer.

10. To make the apartment extra safe, we changed the lock on the new apartment door.

## Exercise 12d

1. If they were to sight him, the astronauts would report that the man in the moon really does exist.

2. When the mixture is well stewed, you drain off the juice.

3. While the students were planning the takeover of the administration building, the police barged in.

4. If it is highly polished, you may slip on the floor.

5. The car proved hard to drive when the driver had been drinking heavily.

6. When parents make use of birth control information, the child can arrive exactly when planned.

7. My bicycle tire went flat while I was hurrying to the dentist.

8. If it is well oiled, I find my motorcycle easier to handle.

9. Although the boy was a minor, the judge suspended the sentence.

10. If it is lost, we shall pay a reward for the ring.

## OMISSIONS AND INCOMPLETE AND ILLOGICAL
## COMPARISONS AND AWKWARDNESS AND OBSCURITY

Incomplete and illogical comparisons frequently detract from the precision and emphasis of expression. Students will frequently neglect to indicate what it is that something is greater than, as in "We have a greater purpose in life," or will gush that something is "so refreshing" or "so beautiful," all of which hints at a comparison but does not bring it out. Frequently the lack of a cogent comparison results in a lack of effective transition. Exercise 14c helps to develop perceptiveness in this particular respect.

The "Basic Sentence Faults" review exercise at the end of section 14 is a particularly good one to determine student facility in the areas of agreement, reference, faulty comparisons, and ineffective sentence transition. If a student can rewrite the exercise sentences effectively, he will have demonstrated a commendable degree of skill in effective sentence composition.

### Exercise 13a

1. The trouble was that the Viet Cong was not prepared to negotiate.

2. This type of novel is difficult to understand.

3. Space travel in the last few years has proved to be expensive but rewarding.

4. He made it seem as if he wanted to be caught.

5. In the past few years, more and more women have been calling for real equality.

6. The estimate from the contractor gave the committee an idea as to how extensive repairs would be.

7. This quality of merchandise would not be sold in a reputable store.

8. I have been trying to decide which make of car I would buy if I had the money.

9. He made a supreme effort in his senior year and graduated with his class.

10. Which brand of toothpaste reduces cavities?

Opinions among instructors will undoubtedly vary as to which of the above sentences would be acceptable in informal speech. It is quite possible that most instructors would accept all of the above sentences except 4 and 9 in most informal speech contexts.

## Exercise 13b

1. Ability to make decisions and to accept discipline mark the difference between a child and an adult.

2. He was fascinated by the idea of skin-diving but he was also afraid of it.

3. She majored in primary education because she was interested in and capable with young children.

4. Being a traveling salesman is difficult, for by the time he gets home he is too tired to talk to or play with his children.

5. I have never ridden in an airplane and I never will ride in one.

6. He finally decided to give up smoking and eventually wound up doing so.

7. Ghetto children deserve a better education and should be getting one.

8. He never dreamed of joining the Peace Corps.

9. The government has spent large sums for defense and, consequently, has fewer resources to help the poor.

10. He wanted to take her home and would have done so if his car had not broken down on the country lane.

1. Although the temperature soared, the public beaches were closed because of water pollution.

2. I have climbed several mountains, among them Mt. McKinley and Mont Blanc. / I have climbed several high mountains such as Mt. McKinley and Mont Blanc.

3. Although the job market is expanding, unskilled workers are unemployed. / The job market is expanding; nevertheless, unskilled workers are unemployed.

4. Many students major in psychology because they want to understand themselves and others better. / Many students major in psychology; the reason is that they want to understand themselves and others better.

5. Although Hemingway lived in Paris, the setting for his stories was Africa. / Hemingway lived in Paris; nevertheless, the setting for his stories was Africa.

6. Although Faulkner wrote of the South, his was a universal message. / Faulkner wrote of the South, but his was a universal message.

7. In spite of the hippies' pledging themselves to nonconformity, they all looked alike and thought alike. / Hippies pledged themselves to nonconformity, but they all looked alike and thought alike.

8. Although premarital sex is gaining acceptance, some people still frown on it. / Premarital sex is gaining acceptance; nevertheless, some people still frown on it.

9. Although candidates make many campaign promises, most of them are not fulfilled. / Candidates make many campaign promises, but most of them are not fulfilled.

10. A young man who sincerely objects to war may refuse to serve in the army in spite of the severe penalties. / Although the penalties are severe, a young man who sincerely objects to war may refuse to serve

in the army.

## Exercise 13d–h

1. He is the best of all Presidents.

2. Rock and roll is more pleasant than other types of music.

3. His face is like that of a movie actor.

4. I like her more than I like her sister.

5. I like James Baldwin better than any other writer.

6. She is as pretty as, if not prettier than, her mother.

7. Humphrey was as well known as, if not more so than, any other Vice-President in history.

8. The business element was more heavily represented than other elements in Nixon's cabinet.

9. Water colors are much easier than other colors.

10. Midwesterners are as friendly as people in any other section in the U.S.

## Exercise 14a-b

1. Although it is smaller, a small town is not much friendlier than a city.

2. Sentence is good as originally written but one way of rewriting it is as follows: He liked her because she was a pretty, blue-eyed blond who was clever, having a green thumb.

3. This would be a much more pleasant world if everyone could do things not because he had to but because he wanted to.

4. College, unlike high school, requires that the student learn to think for himself and use self-discipline.

5. My parents don't understand me--they irk me because they keep telling me to settle down, get a job, get married, and do many other things.

6. Although her face was not attractive, her eyes, which were set apart at just the right distance, were beautiful.

7. The first thing a college freshman learns is how little he knows.

8. His work with delinquent boys wasn't easy at first, but it became easier with each passing day.

9. Most of the aspects about space are quite complicated; others are quite basic.

10. Students have varying problems because they have reasons of their own for coming and live in different places.

## "Basic Sentence Faults" Review Exercise

### (Sections 6 through 14)

1. Harvard generally accepts more students from the Northeast than from other sections. Basis of comparison is not the same.

2. After the frogs had been pickled in formaldehyde for a week, the instructor distributed them for dissection. Modifying phrase refers to wrong word.

3. Because Manhattan is an island, you have to take a bridge to get there from New Jersey. Phrase is omitted which is essential to sentence meaning.

4. The boxers having been battered to a pulp, the referee told them the bout was over. Modifying phrase relates to wrong word.

5. A teen-ager's lecturing to his parents always makes them feel uncomfortable. It is used in an indefinite manner.

6. After a year in Vietnam during which he had grown more used to thatched huts, he had forgotten how

tall skyscrapers were. The modifier <u>after a year in Vietnam</u> is a squinting modifier.

7. He wanted to get there on time with all possible modes of transportation at his disposal. Introductory words <u>however much</u> make original construction a sentence fragment. Also, the coordinate conjunction does not link parallels.

8. The letter was mailed an hour ago in the corner mailbox by the new clerk with the red miniskirt. <u>In the corner mailbox</u> is a misplaced modifier.

9. She likes her better than she does any of the other girls. Original sentence has an incomplete comparison.

10. After being graduated from college, Millicent went to work in the theater as a chorus girl. <u>After being graduated</u> is a misplaced modifier.

MANUSCRIPT MECHANICS

The sections dealing with manuscript mechanics will probably be regarded by many students as the nuisance sections of the book. Manuscript mechanics as such is not an overwhelmingly interesting subject to most writers. Nevertheless, mechanics, even though they may be a very minor aspect of writing, can hardly be regarded as unimportant. After all, unless a manuscript is presented in an attractive format and unless abbreviations are correctly utilized and syllabification is correctly performed, the effect upon the reader can be a distracting one. Also involved on the part of the reader where many mechanical errors occur may be the rather obvious conclusion, obvious to him at least, that if the writer is careless in small matters, he may be careless in more important matters as well. A rather obvious analogy would be that of the individual who spends hours polishing his automobile but who fails to check the oil and water with the result that he ends up with a thing of beauty that doesn't run very far.

## SECTIONS 16-17

## NUMBERS AND ABBREVIATIONS

Abbreviations and numbers can be troublesome in composition writing and the text gives explanations and exercises which should assist in some of the most troublesome aspects in these areas. Instructors may wish to spend some class time in discussion of some of these aspects or may wish only to assign exercises to at least assure student familiarization with these aspects. "The Manuscript" Review Exercise at the end of these sections may prove to be particularly valuable for the latter purpose.

### Exercise 16

1.  John Kennedy was inaugurated on January 20, 1961, at the age of forty-four.

2.  The students' strike lasted ten days.

3.  The satellite model measured 5.19 inches in circumference.

4.  Steven spent two years in the Peace Corps.

5.  The seminar met at 2:30 P.M.

6.  Some students spend as much as ninety-five cents for bus fare daily.

7.  Eighty-five thousand people viewed the President's press conference.

8.  Labor Day is the first Monday in September.

9.  Retail prices were found to be nearly 15 percent higher in the ghetto than in other parts of the city.

10. Nearly four hundred people joined the protest march.

# Exercise 17

1. At 2:00 P.M., the rocket was launched.

2. The President and Ambassador Smith discussed United States policy in the South Pacific.

3. He enrolled in the University of Maine because he liked the New England climate.

4. Mr. Turner spent his August vacation working with a civil rights group in Alabama.

5. Mr. Downs noted the license number of the motorcycle.

6. After years of study in chemistry, he decided to become a doctor.

7. Many mountain passes are closed in the winter in Switzerland.

8. The English professor asked the students to draw on their personal experiences in writing compositions.

9. The urban renewal project will cover the area from Main Street to Michigan Avenue.

10. Next fall the university will offer courses in Black Literature and Black History.

11. The doctor told his patient to take three teaspoons of medicine every two hours.

12. The shortest day of the year is in December.

13. Reverend Paul Crocker's sermons draw upon his training in philosophy.

14. The roads are impassable because of a flood this morning.

15. The captain spent all his dollars on his October furlough.

## SECTION 18

## SYLLABICATION

Syllabication is another area which often gives students trouble. Some general rules have been cited which may prove to be helpful. Many instructors may also want to emphasize the use of the dictionary or a spelling word list as an effective aid to proper syllabication. Spelling word lists which have been marketed by many publishers and which are generally obtainable at a very low cost are sometimes very helpful possessions for students, since such works provide quick assistance in matters of spelling and syllabication.

### Exercise 18

| | | |
|---|---|---|
| drowned | enough | walked |
| swim-mer | twelve | au-to-mo-bile |
| learn-ed | through | ex-er-cise |
| a-brupt | a-cute | open |
| en-ve-lope | ex-president | pre-eminent |

### "Manuscript" Review Exercise

### (Sections 15 through 18)

1. Some stores put a service charge on bills that are not paid within thirty days.

2. I try not to enroll in classes that begin before 10:45 A.M.

3. The vice-president of the student council is occasionally asked to act as chairman of the meetings.

4. The new Center for African Studies will be located at Maple and Main Streets.

5. Three boxtops must accompany every request for a "free" sample.

6. Paperback books, which once sold for a quarter, now cost as much as $5.95.

7. The local movie house will show a Bogart film on the first Monday of every month.

8. Most tourists in New York go to see the Empire State Building first.

9. Some people opposed extending suffrage to eighteen-year-olds.

10. Students should have a voice in such aspects as curriculum development and course selection.

11. The Moore Manufacturing Company gave all old customers a 5 percent reduction.

12. All heavyweight boxers must be over 175 pounds.

13. All perch measuring under five inches must be thrown back into Lake Mendota.

14. Reverend Winters performed the marriage ceremony at the Lutheran Church.

15. Mr. and Mrs. Hone entered their three-year-old filly in the race.

## PUNCTUATION

Punctuation is an area which is frequently troublesome for many students; and sometimes it is a difficult aspect to deal with, since the attitude is often that what is only of a mechanical nature is not greatly important to good writing. Nothing, of course, could be further from the truth. Since good writing stresses accuracy and precision in every respect, it must often rely upon punctuation to help achieve these objectives. Lack of proper punctuation may at times not make a vital difference; at other times it may detract greatly from effective expression.

The Prentice-Hall Handbook for Writers considers the problem of proper punctuation from the perspective of four different functions: end punctuation, internal punctuation, direct quotation punctuation, and word punctuation. A number of exercises are provided both within and at the end of sections relating to each of these functions in addition to a "punctuation" review exercise which covers all aspects of punctuation with which sections 19-30 deal. The latter exercise provides an excellent test of the student's comprehensive understanding of correct punctuation.

SECTION 19

END PUNCTUATION

End punctuation usually does not give students much
difficulty, although some have trouble in distinguishing
between a statement which asks a direct question and a
statement which contains an indirect question. The use of
periods with abbreviations is also sometimes an area of
concern; and, although the text does give examples of proper
usage in this respect, it will often be necessary to stress,
as does the text, that a good dictionary must be consulted
wherever there is doubt whether an abbreviation should be
used.

Exercise 19(1)

1. The reporter asked, "Mr. President, could you
   clarify that remark please?"

2. "Yes," he replied, "let me make that absolutely
   clear."

3. Mr. C. P. Johnson, who formerly worked with the law
   firm of Herrick, Noble, and Snow, is now with the
   U.S. Army.

4. He has a Ph.D. from U.C.L.A., but he earned his
   M.A. from M.I.T.

5. I would live in N.Y.C. if I could afford to live on
   Fifth Ave. and E. 68th St.

6. The NAACP (N.A.A.C.P.) has led the fight for civil
   rights in the U.S., but in recent years S.N.C.C.
   has been gaining more attention.

7. Is Mrs. or Miss the abbreviation for Mistress?

8. "May I quote you on that, Mr. President?" asked the
   reporter.

9. "Oh, why do you insist on quoting everything?" he
   cried.

10.  The guard yelled "Halt!"

## Exercise 19(2)

I remember that.....I used to see Tarzan movies on
Saturday.  White Tarzan used to beat up the black
natives.  I would sit there yelling, "Kill the beasts
...." I was saying:  Kill me.  It was as if a Jewish
boy watched Nazis taking Jews off to concentration
camps and cheered them on.  Today, I want the chief to
beat hell out of Tarzan and send him back to Europe....

MAIN CLAUSES

A knowledge as to how to use the semicolon properly will be invaluable to the student when he is concerned with the punctuation of main clauses.  Actually, the semicolon has only two basic purposes:  separation of independent sentence elements and separation of items in series wherein there is internal punctuation.  Unfortunately, the instructor may find that what is often involved in these respects is not really a misunderstanding of the use of the semicolon as such but an inability to recognize independent and dependent sentence elements.  As such, then, exercises in the use of the semicolon may indicate a need for additional student work in basic sentence structure--in other words, the trouble may be basically a grammatical one rather than a mechanical one.

The colon is another mark of punctuation which can help a student to achieve a great deal of versatility in his writing.  In many instances, the colon can be used interchangeably with the semicolon, although many independent sentence elements do not operate in an amplificatory respect with each other; and where that is true, the semicolon would be required and not the colon.  One way to sharpen the distinction between the colon and semicolon is to emphasize in the case of the semicolon, except where items in series with internal punctuation are involved, that those sentence elements which come before and after the semicolon must be independent.  By comparison, where a colon is involved, what comes before the colon should be an independent element but what comes after it does not have to be.

Sentences dealing with the same subject matter can be worded so as to require either the semicolon or the colon.
   He liked all kinds of vegetables; he particularly liked peas, beans, collards and potatoes.
   He liked all kinds of vegetables:  peas, beans, collards, and potatoes.

In the first of the above sentences, a colon could be substituted for the semicolon and the sentence sense would remain the same.  In the second sentence, though, the semicolon could not be substituted for the colon, since what comes after the colon is only a list of items, and not an independent clause.

1. The morning edition made clear the newspaper's stand: It would back the Republican candidate. 20d

2. Crime rates have been increasing rapidly; therefore, demand for the enforcement of law and order increase rapidly. 20c

3. Every winter the fear of oil shortages is renewed; consequently, more and more voices call for the removal of oil import quotas. 20c

4. Student interest in colleges and universities has declined and, in some cases, almost disappeared; still, there is great continuing need for change in higher education. 20c

5. The Senator's record showed that he had consistently voted against every civil rights bill introduced during his term of office; so the voters turned against him in the next election. 20b

6. Space scientists are highly knowledgeable in engineering, physics, and mathematics; however, they may not be capable of replacing a burnt-out light bulb at home.

7. During the period around 1960, interiors of buildings were more ornately decorated; but some interiors, notably those in the IBM and Winnematic buildings, clung to the old, simple modern look. 21a 20a,23b

8. Edward Albee commemorated the great blues singer Bessie Smith in his play The Death of Bessie Smith, although the emphasis of the play is on racial prejudice and not the blues. 21c

9. The difference between men and women is a simple one: Men earn the money and women spend it. 20d

10. Many scientists believe that marijuana is no more harmful or addictive than alcohol; nevertheless, alcohol is legal while marijuana is not. 20c

1. Public opinion polls indicated that Mrs. Kennedy's popularity had declined after her marriage to Onassis; still it was not clear whether this was the sole reason.

2. European housewives shop daily; consequently, they do not have left-over food to throw away.

3. Student demonstrations were becoming increasingly violent; school administrators adopted a "get tough" attitude.

4. There were some congested areas on the highway; still, for the most part, traffic flowed smoothly.

5. The witness was positive that these were the men-- they had rushed into the bank in broad daylight and held the employees at gunpoint.

6. Strong efforts must be made to bridge the gap between the races, or this nation will be split into two separate societies.

7. Common sense is not a very common quality; therefore, those who possess it are usually sought after.

8. At that time, the Smiths thought nothing of the occasional signs of oil on the floor of the garage although they recalled later that their oil tank needed constant refilling.

9. The thundershower ended as quickly as it had begun, the spectators filed back into their seats, and the baseball game was resumed.

10. The reporters waited patiently for the President until noon; then they began to batter the press secretary with questions.

## SECTION 21

### SUBORDINATE PHRASES AND CLAUSES

When an introductory expression occurs before a main clause, little punctuation trouble usually occurs. This is particularly true if the student has learned to recognize the conjunctive adverbs and verbals and to realize that if sentences begin with some words or phrases a comma is invariably required. Troubles are encountered, though, where the types of expressions that often precede the main clauses are inserted after main clauses. In such instances, in addition to observing the instructions set forth in section 21c, the voice itself can often be used as a guide to determine whether or not punctuation is required. Note in the following sentences how the voice inflection either does or does not indicate emphasis.

There is nothing to worry about unless it rains (no real concern on the part of the speaker that rain is expected).

There is nothing to worry about, unless it rains (a sense of foreboding on the part of the speaker that it will rain).

### Exercise 21(1)

1. Having completed a course in gourmet cookery, she began to give a series of large dinner parties.

2. After visiting several mental institutions, I became interested in pursuing a career in mental health.

3. For all the talk of "redeeming social value," most of the new films and plays are really involved with prurience.

4. In spite of their best efforts to keep up with the problems of youth, most modern parents are at a loss to understand their own children.

5. Because of the high incidence of fatal injuries, motorcyclists in most states are required to wear helmets.

6. Few white people know, and even fewer try to learn how difficult the life of the average black American has been.

7. To one who is interested in farming, land has beauty and character.

8. After he had finished medical school and had been an intern for two years, he began his medical research.

9. Sheila is interested in nursing because it gives her a feeling of being needed. No comma necessary.

10. As we expected, the fighting in South Vietnam continued after the cease-fire agreement.

## Exercise 21(2)

1. When the exam sheet was placed in front of him, he realized how much he had neglected to study. Comma is needed after introductory adverbial clause.

2. Sentence is punctuated correctly.

3. Sentence is punctuated correctly.

4. During his final exile on the remote island of St. Helena, Napoleon was poisoned, many believe. Commas are needed after beginning participial phrase and before explanatory phrase.

5. His program rejected by the French people, De Gaulle resigned the presidency. Comma is required after absolute construction.

6. Annoyed by the coughing in the audience, John Barrymore once stalked off the stage during a performance. Comma is required after beginning participial phrase.

7. After the assassination of President Kennedy, gun-control was proposed, but it was defeated. Comma is needed after introductory adverb clause and comma is required between main clauses.

8. After they had followed their guru to India, the Beatles decided that there was no place like home.

Comma is required after beginning clause introduced by subordinating conjunction <u>after</u>.

9. Having lost the race for governor of California in 1962, Nixon vowed he would never again seek public office. Comma is required after participial phrase.

10. Sentence is punctuated correctly.

## NONRESTRICTIVES AND OTHER PARENTHETICAL ELEMENTS; ITEMS IN A SERIES; FINAL APPOSITIVES AND SUMMARIES

In addition to the other guidelines discussed by the text, the voice may also be used in many instances to determine whether the expression is nonrestrictive and hence requires setting off by commas or whether it is restrictive and does not need punctuation. In such instances, the voice will invariably drop before and after a nonrestrictive expression but will not do so where a restrictive expression is involved.

The dash is another very useful mark of punctuation. However, once some students learn that a dash can be used for dramatic emphasis, their flair for the dramatic may result in dash-studded writing efforts. Instructors, consequently, may have to emphasize repeatedly the judicious use of all writing devices. On the other hand, the contrasting emphasis obtained by the substitution of the dash for the parenthesis, or vice versa, may be pondered by a consideration of sentences such as the following:

> Joe Doakes (the best football player in the conference) was a straight A student.

> Joe Doakes--the best football player in the conference--was a straight A student.

Similarly, a better appreciation of the need for proper punctuation can be achieved when modifiers become either restrictive or nonrestrictive according as to whether commas are or are not used. Sentences such as the following can sometimes help to prove this point.

> All male students who fail their courses will be drafted.

> All male students, who fail their courses, will be drafted.

> Women who can't drive properly should keep off the road.

> Women, who can't drive properly, should keep off

the road.

## Exercise 22(1)

1. The President defended, or rather tried to defend, his policy of not spending money appropriated by Congress.

2. Clause beginning with "who drafted" is restrictive and hence no punctuation is required.

3. John L. Lewis, an aggressive union leader, was a self-educated man.

4. The result of her attempt to win him back was, as you can guess, humiliating.

5. Ronald Reagan, after a successful career in the movies, began an equally successful career in politics. Dashes could be used to set off appositive to emphasize the movie experience.

6. Queen Elizabeth II, ignoring the threats of Welsh nationalists, invested her son as Prince of Wales.

7. Clause beginning with "who know" is restrictive and hence no punctuation is required.

8. Although he is still a very young man, Julian Bond is being watched by older politicians.

9. Choosing their words carefully, the student leaders explained to the administration officials the nature of their grievances.

10. Few Americans know very much about our nearest and best neighbor, Canada.

## Exercise 22(2)

1. Uranium, which is one of our most valuable elements, is capable of fission; therefore it is necessary in hydrogen bombs.

2. An atomic reactor may be used for destructive

72

purposes, but it may also be used to benefit mankind.

3. Heart transplants, once confined to science fic-
   tion, are now becoming standard medical practice.

4. U.S. policy is, as you know, to prevent the prolif-
   eration of atomic weapons.

5. The Christmas shopping season, which all merchants
   look forward to, begins earlier and earlier each
   year.

6. Traveling in Asia, if one is willing to experiment
   with new foods, can be a very exciting experience.

7. Most dress designers expected, and some were trying
   to encourage, women to become bored with mini-
   skirts.

8. Black studies programs, although they are being
   instituted primarily for black students, will prove
   interesting to white students as well.

9. The seizure of the Pueblo by the North Koreans,
   unexpected and unprecedented, set off waves of
   international alarm.

10. Sentence is correctly punctuated as it stands.


## Exercise 23

1. Among the countries I visited last summer were
   Rumania, Bulgaria, and Poland -- all behind the
   Iron Curtain.

2. The telephone operator reported that there was no
   33 Pine Drive in Austin, that there is no Michael
   Stone listed at any other address, and that there
   is no telephone exchange beginning with 254 in that
   area.

3. To pursue a career in the theater, one must have
   talent, a great deal of energy, and a supreme
   confidence in himself.

4. If TV commercials are to be believed, the American

dream consists of a new car, a color television set, and a mate who uses an effective mouthwash.

5. Fletcher Christian's men, after taking over the _Bounty_, seemingly disappeared from the face of the earth; nearly twenty years were to pass before their hiding place was found.

6. Taking off his wrinkled old white cap, lowering his tattered black umbrella, and scraping his tennis shoes on the doormat, he rang the bell.

7. The sculpture was dominated by two large poles overhanging several round objects that appeared to represent a crowd of people, but we were not certain if our guess was correct.

8. Medical insurance plans are not keeping pace with rising medical costs; the hardest hit are the poor and the aged.

9. After he left office, former President Johnson said he was going back to Texas to rediscover the joy of hunting, fishing, playing with his grandchildren, and just relaxing.

10. The John Hancock in Boston is the tallest building on the mainland of North America, but only if one remembers that Manhattan Island is not, strictly speaking, part of the mainland.


Exercise 24

1. Of all the things I relish eating, this is first-- steak.

2. She came back from New York a new woman: her hair was bleached, her face lifted, and her nose short- ened.

3. The mechanical errors many students have the most difficulty mastering are run-on sentences, punctu- ation with semicolons and colons, and reference of pronouns.

4. Of all the countries I visited last summer, the one I liked best was Greece--that's the one country I

think I could live in.

5. If you live in a city, you must observe speed
limits; therefore, it seems pointless to buy a
sports car.

6. National boundaries in Africa do not coincide with
tribal boundaries; therefore it is inevitable that
these new nations must endure some internal fric-
tions during the first few years of independence.

7. The Maoist doctrine of constant revolution finds
little acceptance in Europe--even the Soviet Union
is made uneasy by it.

8. The staunchest support for Red China does not come
from any of the major Communist nations in Europe,
but from the smallest and least significant--Alba-
nia.

9. It was a sad day for Brooklyn when the Dodgers
moved to Los Angeles, but now Brooklynites' attention is focused on a new favorite--the Mets.

10. Aging movie stars talk of "waiting for the right
script"--the truth is probably that they haven't
been offered a role in years.

SUPERFLUOUS INTERNAL PUNCTUATION

Sometimes, one of the most difficult student punctuation errors to correct is overpunctuation.  Some students
seem to have a compulsive tendency to automatically insert
commas in sentences where commas are definitely out of
place.  This type of student will frequently write sentences
such as the following:
>My car is, for sale.
>He hit the ball, a long distance.
>A beautiful girl, enrolled in the course.
>He disliked, every moment of his army career.

The tendency to inject commas between subjects and
verbs, verbs and complements, verbs and object, and integral
units of sentences may be indicative only of a lack of
knowledge of proper punctuation; it may, on the other hand,
be indicative of a lack of knowledge of effective sentence
structure.

### Exercise 25

1. The standard way of cleaning mines is for a
   minesweeper to detonate them from a safe distance.

2. The Constitution is a safeguard that protects certain
   rights, no matter what public opinion may be at the
   time.

3. Too many prophets of doom are scaring us by telling
   us that pesticides will destroy the land, and that
   burning fuel will change our weather and climate.

4. However we interpret it, there is no doubt that
   "American Pie" is one of the most popular songs of
   the year.

5. Nobody knows what the men who work under the Secretary
   of State really think of him, or of his policies.

6. Nudity on the public stage, once undreamed of but now

commonly accepted, may eventually run out its course
and be received only with apathy.

7. The Job Corps, a federal program to aid the uneducated
and unskilled, was forced, because of a reduced budget,
to make proportionate reductions in its services.

8. The senator replied slowly because he had not expected
the question, and he really didn't know what to say.

9. The United States is slowly taking over the world,
not with guns, but with Coca-Cola and television
reruns.

10. The disenchantment with urban renewal stems from the
fact that frequently it is merely a matter of building
new slums to replace the old.

## "Internal Punctuation" Review Exercises

### (Sections 20 through 25)

### Exercise A

1. The President, critics say, has gained too much power
in foreign affairs at the expense of the Senate.

2. A quiet stretch of Sudbury farmland, set behind a row
of tidy typical colonials, is the setting of the
story.

3. Preoccupied by the war in Indochina, The United States
has been unable to give enough attention to problems
in other parts of the world.

4. The following courses will be offered by the English
Department in the Summer Term:  Modern American Novel,
Advanced Composition, Emerson and Hawthorne, and
Poetry of the Seventeenth Century.

5. As the chairman stated, the present at large method
of electing city officials results in over-represen-
tation of certain areas, under-respresentation of
others.

6. Mr. Goldberg, who was once U.S. Ambassador to the UN,

was also once an associate justice of the Supreme Court.

7.  There's only one problem involved in "doing your own thing": that's that everyone else may want to do his own thing as well.

8.  It's relatively easy to borrow money -- (or ;) it's much harder to pay it back.

9.  Jealousy, a debilitating emotion, can wreck a relationship; for without genuine trust, there can be no real love.

10. There is some evidence that Christopher Columbus was not the first European to visit America; recent discoveries reveal that there may have been Viking settlements on the northeastern tip of the continent.

Exercise B

## Science and Human Values

A semicolon is employed after science in the third sentence to separate two independent clauses. A comma is also used after truth to provide emphasis to the following correlative phrase. Step by step is set off by commas because it is a nonrestrictive expression. In the last sentence, not given is separated from found with a comma to provide emphasis, and it is followed by a comma because it is the termination of an introductory subordinate clause. The comma after action is inserted because the construction of which action is a part is also a subordinate clause. Parentheses enclose the phrase beginning with and because the phrase interrupts the structure of the sentence.

## Desert Solitaire

In the first sentence, the author uses brackets to indicate who the they is to whom he is referring. Commas are used to set off the nonrestrictive expression, some... later, and a colon is employed after extinguished because following it is amplifying material concerning what has already been discussed in the sentence. The series of short questions following achieve dramatic impact and act as a prefatory structuring device leading up to the subsequent explanation. A semicolon is use in the sentence beginning with The old to separate two independent clauses

and, in the same sentence, a comma separates the first two
of three items in the series.  In the following sentence,
commas are used to set off the nonrestrictive expression
beginning with <u>an emigration</u> and a comma separates <u>sudden</u>
and <u>panicky</u> to indicate that late adjectives modify <u>flight</u>.
The effect of the dashes in the sentence beginning with
<u>In almost all of the cliff dwellings</u> is the emphasize the
items contained within the dashes.  In the next sentence,
a comma is used after <u>dead</u> to achieve emphasis between the
independent clause and the following subordinate expression.
In the last two sentences, commas are used to set off the
nonrestrictive expression beginning with <u>having no</u>, and to
provide emphasis in the subordinate expression beginning
with <u>associated</u>.

## Confusion and Disorder

A colon in the first sentence separates a basic
statement from following amplifying material; commas
separate items in series and separate a subordinate
clause terminating in <u>clay</u> from the following independent
clause; in turn, a semicolon after <u>rapidly</u> separates two
dependent-independent clause constructions; in the latter
part of the sentence, commas are again used to separate
items in series and, after <u>music</u>, to separate a dependent
from an independent clause.  In the next to the last
sentence, a comma is used in conjunction with the
coordinating conjunction <u>but</u> to separate independent
clauses.  In the last sentence, a colon follows a basic
statement followed by explanatory material.  Commas are
also used here to separate independent clauses and to
emphasize the division at <u>for</u> between the preceding
independent and the following dependent constructions.

# SECTION 26

## PUNCTUATION OF QUOTED MATERIAL

The punctuation of quoted material sometimes causes difficulty for students who cannot distinguish between a direct and an indirect quotation.  Where this difficulty is manifested, instructors may want to assign additional work.  Quotations within larger quotations, how to refer to a word used in a special sense, and the placement of commas, periods, and other marks of punctuation either within or without the final quotation mark, are other punctuation uses that the instructor may want to emphasize, since these are areas in which many student errors in punctuation are often made.

### Exercise 26

1. The letter said tartly, "The fault is not with our product but with your skin; it appears to be super-sensitive."

2. "Perhaps you might like to do a study of the sexual imagery in Shakespeare," the professor suggested.

3. "How long have you noticed this condition?" the doctor asked.

4. As the history professor said in class yesterday, "There is no real evidence that Marie Antoinette ever said 'Let them eat cake!'"

5. He said, "When the policeman asked me, 'Where's the fire?' I felt like giving him an equally sarcastic answer."

6. The song "Aquarius" is from the controversial musical Hair.

7. Arthur Schlesinger, Jr. says John Stuart Mill wrote a century ago:  "The greatness of England is now all collective; individually small, we appear capable of anything great only by our habit of combining."

8. The salesgirl said, "Madam, I would exchange this sweater, but," she added, "It has already been worn."

9. One day, just as I was going to Rahul's house, I heard her shouting outside the door of the study. "The director is a busy man!" she was shouting. She had her back against the door and held her arms stretched out; M. stood in front of her and his head was lowered, "Day after day you come and eat his life up!" she said.

10. I climbed up in the bar yelling, "Walsh, I'm shot! I'm shot!" I could feel the blood running down my leg. Walsh, the fellow who operated the fish-and-chips joint, pushed me off the bar and onto the floor. I couldn't move now, but I was still completely conscious. Walsh was saying, "Git outta here, kid. I ain't got no time to play." A woman was screaming, mumbling something about the Lord, and saying, "Somebody done shot that poor child."

## SECTIONS 27-30

## ITALICS; CAPITALS; APOSTROPHE; HYPHEN

Word punctuation involving italics, capitalization, and possession often gives trouble. All of these are admittedly minor aspects of writing; yet, mistakes in word punctuation detract from overall quality of writing and often give the reader the impression he is reading the work of a very careless or a very unsophisticated writer. In this connection, it is interesting to note that use of the word "it's" as the possessive of "it" is probably one of the four or five most misspelled words in the English language. Similarly, "their," which is supposed to indicate the possessive of "they," is a very widely misspelled word. Of course, what is really involved here is most probably not misspelling at all but a lack of understanding of how to form the possessive of these words. Again, an understanding of basic structure can prevent the making of embarrassing errors in writing; the attitude that such errors are inconsequential would be like saying that a scratch on a brand new automobile is of no consequence to a prospective buyer.

## Exercise 27

1. James Earl Jones, the eminent black actor, received a Tony award for his Broadway performance in The Great White Hope.

2. H.M.S. Queen Elizabeth, for years the flagship of the Cunard Line, was finally retired from service.

3. Are you supposed to pronounce the p in coup d'etat?

4. Some Americans use the word simpatico as though it meant sympathetic, but its meaning is really closer to that of the English word charming.

5. Is T. S. Eliot's "The Wasteland" included in The Oxford Book of English Verse?

6. His travels had brought him greater understanding of himself and just a touch of savoir-faire.

7. <u>Webster's</u> <u>Third</u> <u>New</u> <u>International</u> <u>Dictionary</u> lists more than half a dozen pronunciations of <u>lingerie</u>.

8. I am constantly forgetting what <u>eclectic</u> means.

9. New Englanders tend to add an <u>r</u> to words that end in <u>a</u> and to omit the <u>r</u> in words that do end in <u>r</u>.

10. Thus in Boston, <u>Cuba</u> becomes <u>Cuber</u>, while <u>river</u> becomes <u>riva</u>.


Exercise 28

1. Last summer he worked with the Job Corps, which was part of a larger federal program.

2. The Reverend Martin Luther King, Jr. first came to public attention as a leader of the civil rights sit-ins in the South.

3. The late Robert Kennedy had been Attorney General of the United States before being elected senator from the state of New York.

4. It has been predicted that power in the U.N. will eventually shift from the Security Council to the General Assembly.

5. The Boston Symphony Orchestra is not to be confused with the Boston Pops Orchestra.

6. All math majors who were preparing to teach elementary school students were required by the math department to take courses in the new math.

7. The Organization of the American States is designed to encourage cooperation and understanding among the nations of the Western Hemisphere.

8. Michael O'Hara, president of the student congress, addressed the meeting.

9. Many of the Aberdeen Angus cattle come from the state of Nebraska.

10. It was the fall of the Roman Empire which ushered in the Middle Ages.

1. One of my most prized possessions is the Supremes' first record album.

2. It's hard to believe that in a country as rich as ours, some people still go to bed hungry every night.

3. The chairman's secretary has assured all members of the department that they'll have their class schedules in two weeks' time.

4. Most modern cities haven't the resources with which to keep up with their expanding populations.

5. He had asked for a month's leave of absence, but he was allowed to take only the three days' sick leave that were due him.

6. Sentence is punctuated correctly as originally given.

7. What's the point of experimenting with mind-expanding drugs when they can do terrible damage to one's mind?

8. A rock group's career, as show business goes, is relatively short.

9. The greatest years of The New Yorker were those under Harold Ross' editorship.

10. It's hard to keep up with the Joneses when you don't have Mr. Jones' income.


Exercise 30

1. In choosing a car, you should remember that a well-tuned motor is more important than white-wall tires.

2. He boasts that he is self-made and self-educated but he forgets to add that he is also self-centered.

3. The life-long dream of most Americans is fulfilled

when they move into a four-bedroom house with a two-car garage.

4. He changed a twenty-dollar bill into twenty dollar bills and distributed them among the children.

5. In a well-planned maneuver, the students re-entered the administration building and retook their position in the corridors.


Exercise 27-30(1)

1. Ex-Governor Spiro Agnew of Maryland became Vice-President of the United States.

2. _Playboy_ magazine is designed to appeal to the would-be man-about-town type.

3. Sentence is correct as originally written.

4. It's a well known fact that most old age pensions are inadequate for the present-day needs of senior citizens.

5. It's hard to believe that old-timer was once All-American fullback of 1910.


Exercise 27-30(2)

1. Steinbeck's novel, _The Grapes of Wrath_, written in the 1930's, helped him to win the Nobel Prize for literature.

2. Barbra Streisand's first big break in show business was in the Broadway play, _I Can Get It for You Wholesale_.

3. That young man's heart is not yours, nor mine, nor hers.

4. The four American delegates' carefully prepared proposal was rejected by the Soviet Union's spokesman.

5. Long before Israel was declared a nation, its people had yearned for a home of their own.

6. Although eighteen-year-olds are subject to the draft, my brother's friend wasn't called until he was twenty-one years old.

7. The fall semester began mid-September this year so that freshmen could complete their pre-entrance orientation program.

8. All surviving members of the <u>Pueblo's</u> crew were besieged by fact-seeking newsmen.

9. The Huntley-Brinkley Show is one of NBC's major attractions.

10. The four-cylinder sixty-horsepower car wasn't able to pull Jones's custom-built limousine out of the ditch.

"Punctuation" Review Exercises

(Sections 19 through 30)

Exercise A

1. The most famous sentence from President Kennedy's inaugural speech is the one that begins, "Ask not what your country can do for you...."

2. Her term paper consisted of nothing more than a series of quotations from the works of Shakespeare, Marlowe, and Milton strung together with some ill thought-out and half-baked comments of her own.

3. De Gaulle's chief virtues or faults, as the case may be, were a supreme self-confidence, an inability to compromise, and a strong resistance to any kind of criticism of his or his appointees' ideas.

4. Something must be wrong with the school system; it has a tremendous number of dropouts and truants.

5. I have just received an unexpected letter from the Director of the Bureau of Internal Revenue.

6. Although I am not a member of the Democratic party, I am very democratic in my relationships with people.

7. Ruth wanted a Pontiac; Francis, a Ford; Donna, a Chrysler; and Alice, a Raleigh bicycle.

8. The late Will Rogers' favorite saying was "I've never met a man I didn't like."

9. At least two states allow eighteen-year-olds to vote. Kentucky, I think, is one. Or is it Georgia?

10. Judy Garland is best remembered for her role in the 1930's film The Wizard of Oz.

11. During the 1968 Presidential campaign, Spiro Agnew's remark, "When you've seen one slum, you've seen them all," considerably distressed his running mate.

12. The students were asked to read two books, Candy and Portnoy's Complaint; but they failed to find in either any so-called "redeeming social significance."

13. Does anyone remember who said, "Absolute power corrupts absolutely"?

14. I make it a point to read the New York Times every day and Life magazine every week; only rarely, however, do I get around to Time or Newsweek.

15. "You can't do that!" she cried hysterically. "You can't! You can't!"


## Exercise B

1. It is astonishing in retrospect how constantly and boldly this Irish Catholic President--this young man so publicly committed to things like patriotism and public affairs--lampooned politicians. politics, notions, men, systems, myths, himself, even his church. When the Wall Street Journal criticized Nixon, Kennedy said it was like L'Obsservatore Romano criticizing the Pope, and Speaker John McCormack denies that Kennedy called him archbishop. "He called me Cardinal," McCormack recalls. When the Vatican implied some criticism of Kennedy's campaign effort to prove himself free of papal influence, Kennedy said ruefully to a pair of

reporters, "Now I understand why Henry the Eighth set up his own church."

2. "Trip" describes the psychedelic experience very well. "It is gratuitous, an extra day in the week," one saying goes, and the sense of this experience being unearned is perhaps the common feature of all the attitudes that have grown up around it. It shapes the disbelief of those who have not experienced it; and, paradoxically, it confirms the belief that something quite so rich in life experience must somehow always be a gift and unmerited. The view of ordinary life is nearly always altered after a trip, but this does not mean the style of post-psychedelic life is set or naturally follows. Egos are still distinct twins in their variety; and the egoless, the genuine LSD head, can't really be said to have returned from his trip. You can't bring the universe home with you; perhaps all you can do is choose your home.

3. The other pitfall blocking the path of the New Left is the culture's skill at amiably absorbing all manner of rebels and turning them into celebrities. To be a radical in America today is like trying to punch your way out of a cage made of marshmallow: every thrust at the jugular draws not blood, but sweet success; every hack at the roots draws not retaliation, but fame and affluence. The culture's insatiable thirst for novelty and titillation insured Leroi Jones television interviews, Norman Mailer million dollar royalties, and Paul Goodman fat paychecks as a government consultant. Yesterday's underground becomes today's vaudeville and tomorrow's cliche. If the draft, super patriots, and the Justice Department don't wreck the New Left, masscult may kill it with kindness and then deposit its carcass in the cemetery of celebrities alongside of Jane Holzer, Liberace, and Jack Kerouac.

Exercise C

1. I've seen the play <u>Hello Dolly</u> twice, but I still find its plot fascinating. "It's" is not possessive of "it is" but the contraction of "it is."

2. Sentence is correct as it is originally written.

3. Isn't it time we all ignored our own personal problems and co-operated with one another in making this world a better place to live in? Contraction for "Is not" is "Isn't"; Sentence construction is in nature of a question.

4. She watches television all day long and in the evening too. Sentence is not long enough to warrant internal punctuation; also, except where a series with internal punctuation is involved, a semicolon is used only to separate independent sentence elements.

5. Should one judge a candidate from the speeches he makes? From the printed matter he distributes? Or, from the ideas he generates? Question mark is an end-stop mark of punctuation which is required here after constructions phrased as questions.

6. Sentence is correctly punctuated as it stands.

7. The President's daughters' (daughter's) activities are always reported in the press; so are his wife's. Apostrophes are required to show possession. "So are his wife's" is an independent sentence element and hence requires a semicolon to separate it from rest of sentence.

8. I think I recognize that actor--wasn't he on the television show <u>My Three Sons</u>? Dash here best sets off the turn in direction of the thought.

9. "I wanted to make that perfectly clear," the President said. "Have I made it so?" Quotation marks are required to set off the exact words uttered by another. Period indicates end of first complete sentence.

10. As one pundit once observed of Senator Dirksen, "He certainly couldn't be accused of using any greasy kid stuff!" Quotation could be written without exclamation point, depending upon the assumption that is made relative to speaker's tone of voice.

LARGER ELEMENTS

One of the most difficult aspects in a composition involves subject matter. Many students, left to their own devices, will take the position that there is really nothing
they want to write about or nothing to write about that they
want to devote much attention to. Obviously, if a means can
be found to interest them in a subject, the chances of their
writing effectively will be enhanced considerably. In this
connection, since a list of suggested subjects will often be
helpful, paragraph 31a with its accompanying exercises may
assist the student to explore specific facets of a broad
general subject. Another method that many instructors have
utilized successfully is to require students to write compositions based upon reading assignments. This method can, in
some instances, provide subject matter for which the student
can legitimately be held responsible and will often accomplish the additional objective of furthering his knowledge
concerning a specific area. In other instances, reading
material can provoke interest in matters of student concern
and motivate individual responses to issues which have been
raised.

Writing in generalities is an occupational hazard of
student composition writing. There are many reasons for
this and many ways in which to attack the problem. Initially, the student should be assisted to select a subject which
he can explore fully in a freshman composition of conventional length. The emphasis here, consequently, must be on
saying a lot about a little rather than a little about a
lot. The key again would seem to be a very thorough knowledge of the prospective subject. A person who really understands the subject of football, for example, will be able to
say a great deal about the types of blocks that an offensive
tackle will be required to make--on such a subject, he can
go into very great detail upon one narrow phase of the game,
and this is exactly the sort of thing that is generally desired in a conventional length freshman composition. Similarly, a student who knows firearms thoroughly may be able
to write a detailed description of how to clean a pistol--
he will be able to say a great deal upon what is a very
limited phase of gunnery.

# SECTION 31

## THE WHOLE COMPOSITION

The thesis statement is a device that has been effectively used by many students as a means of insuring that they really understand what they are about in writing a composition and of assuring themselves that they "keep on the track" in dealing with their subject. The ability to write a good thesis statement does not come easily; for this reason, many instructors may find it desirable to spend a great deal of time on this subject. One of the best ways of achieving this ability is to write summary statements of paragraphs of other people's compositions. Exercises 31c (3-4) provide a good basis for mastering this skill. Many instructors will also find it desirable to require the submission of a thesis statement with each composition their students write. Oftentimes, an analysis of the student's composition from the perspective of his thesis statement will provide a basis whereby the student can be appraised of a tendency to wander or of a failure to provide concrete substantiatory details.

Outlining is another area that many instructors will want to emphasize, since it requires intensive student application to the very important prewriting process. Proper utilization of the outlining process requires that a student think through his subject very carefully prior to writing, that he have in mind the points he wants to discuss, and that he decide in advance the order in which he wants to discuss these points. At the same time, outlining requires that specific points be made concerning broader aspects of the subject and, hence, helps the student provide detailed information concerning aspects of discussion. Many instructors have found that very constructive results can be achieved by requiring that outlines which have been developed to at least three stages be submitted with compositions. Another effective instructional technique is to require the submission of a detailed outline for evaluation, comment, and revision prior to the time that the composition is written.

What type of an outline should be used is, of course, a matter of discretion, although many instructors prefer the sentence outline for two reasons: first, it requires the student to think the subject through more thoroughly than if he is required to prepare a topic outline; second, a side benefit accrues in the sharpening of the student's skills in composing short, precise, to-the-point sentences. To emphasize the various aspects of tense, voice, mood, and number consistency, another aspect that can be emphasized very strongly with the sentence outline is parallel structure--a writing technique that is often very helpful in assisting the student to achieve maximum economy and vigor of expression. In this connection, class discussion of the sample sentence outline on page 215 of the text can often be profitable. As the outline is discussed, sentences can be revised to employ active or passive voice, depending upon the original construction. Exercises 31g (1-3) should be valuable aids in achieving student ability to outline, particularly if the additional requirement is imposed relative to exercise 31g (1) that outlines be prepared in sentence outline form.

Another instructional device that is often quite effective in assisting students to understand better the principles of good outlining is for the instructor to select an

appropriate subject and then to outline it in class, utilizing either the blackboard or a projector in the process. An
example of the type of outline that can be used in this
respect is the following:

## FINDING A SUMMER JOB

I. Introduction: A student has an option as to what he may
do during the summer.

    A. He may take it easy.
       1. Loafing is a lot of fun.
       2. Doing nothing involves little effort.

    B. He may get a summer job.
       1. Working includes many worthwhile experiences.
       2. Working enables him to make money.

II. The student has available to him several methods of
finding a job.
    A. He can study the newspapers.
       1. The want ad sections list many job opportunities.
       2. He can acquaint himself with firms through their
          advertising.

    B. He can utilize the college employment service.
       1. Many employers advertise for help through the
          above service.
       2. He can advertise his services through this
          agency.

III. Conclusion: The student should select his position on
the basis of several factors.

    A. He should consider his basic interests.
       1. He should try to get a job which interests him.
       2. He should try to get a job he is qualified for.

    B.  He should consider the conditions of the employment.
        1.  Pay is important, but it is not everything.
        2.  A congenial environment is very important, too.


    As the instructor lists the various headings and sub-
headings in the outline, he can illustrate to the class that
something akin to a mathematical process is involved in outlining.  In other words, the subheadings under any heading
or other subheading must add up to the heading or subheadings above in the sense that every subpoint must relate to
the part or subheading above it (e.g. $I = A + (1 + 2) +
B + (1 + 2)$.  Such a procedure can very effectively bring
out that proper outlining insures that the writer keep to
his subject.  It can also illustrate that utilization of
subheadings requires that the various facets be explored on
a progressively more and more specific basis--the more subheadings, the more specific becomes the outline.

    If the sample outline reproduced above is discussed,
the instructor should be careful to point out that its
utilization is to illustrate three aspects:  outline development to three stages, parallel structure in an outline,
and the achievement of unified writing by showing the relationship of all subheadings to subheadings and main headings above them.  As a guide to the writing of an actual
paper, however, the sample outline would be seriously deficient in that the body is developed only to the same extent
as is the introduction and conclusion; and this, of course,
would be undesirable since the body of a composition should
normally be at least three to four times as long as either
the introduction or the conclusion.

    Another instructional device that can be effectively
employed at this stage is to discuss from an outline, copies
of which have been provided to the students, how a paper can
be written.  A copy of an outline which might be prepared
for such a purpose is reproduced below for informational
purposes.

I. Introduction:  Writing is important and its techniques warrant discussion.
   A. Writing rates in importance with reading and mathematics.
      1. Writing is performed by almost everyone in daily life.
      2. Even people with limited educations need to know how to write.
   B. Freshman composition will be discussed.
      1. Discussion will be with respect to the 500-word theme.
      2. The three major parts of a paper, the introduction, the body and the conclusion, will be discussed in that order.

II. Do the following things in the introduction of the paper.
   A. Catch reader's attention by one of the following means:
      1. Show importance of subject,
      2. Use a startling statement or fact,
      3. Use a question,
      4. Or use a short incident or happening.
   B. Indicate purposes of paper.
      1. A paper has an overall purpose.
      2. A paper has a specific purpose.
   C. Signal the structure or organization of the subject matter.
      1. Indicate parts of the subject.
      2. Indicate the order of discussion.

III. The body of the paper will involve organization and development.
   A. Consider two aspects in organization.
      1. Break subject down into parts to be discussed.

2. Decide order of parts of the subject according to one of following:
   a. Chronological order,
   b. Space order,
   c. Cause and effect order,
   d. Or common sense order.
B. Develop subject properly
   1. Provide necessary information to make known something that is not known.
   2. Select one or more of the following means of development:
      a. Listing,
      b. Repeating,
      c. Giving examples,
      d. Comparing,
      e. Or defining.

IV. The conclusion will involve various aspects.
   A. It will bring composition to a close by one of two methods.
      1. Use transitional phrases such as "in conclusion".
      2. Convey through content that composition is being concluded.
   B. It should restate and resummarize.
      1. Briefly restate purpose of paper.
      2. Briefly resummarize important points.
   C. It should indicate significance of what has been described.
      1. Emphasize importance to reader.
      2. Emphasize applicability of items discussed to a larger context.

V. Conclusion: The college freshman can improve his writing ability.
   A. The purpose of this paper has been twofold.
      1. General characteristics of expository writing have been discussed.
      2. The 500-word theme has been discussed.

B. A quick review of the steps and parts of the writing process is as follows:

1. Select the subject.
2. Determine the purpose for writing.
3. Organize the subject by dividing it into its component parts and arranging these parts in logical order.
4. In introduction, catch reader's attention, make purpose for writing clear, and indicate order of discussion.
5. In body, develop parts of subject by such devices as listing, repeating, giving examples, comparing and defining.
6. In conclusion, reaffirm purposes, briefly summarize important points and indicate significance to reader of what has been discussed.

The students should be advised ahead of time to follow the outline as the instructor proceeds in his discussion and to note how he utilizes the various outline headings and subheadings as a springboard for expansion of his discourse, filling in many other details as he goes along. The point can be made in this connection that the purpose of an outline is to provide only the skeleton upon which the composition itself is to be based, and that the actual fleshing in of details occurs in the composition itself. This can be an important point insofar as many students are concerned, since many will tend to overprepare as far as the outline is concerned, resulting in the outline's being about as long as the composition itself--something, of course, that goes beyond the purpose of the outline.

The prewriting process will probably have to be greatly emphasized insofar as many students are concerned. This stems from the fact that even though most students can see the purpose of advance preparation in other fields of endeavor, they often seem to think as far as writing is concerned that all they have to do is provide a favorable environment for writing, invoke the muse, and by some magical method thoughts will automatically be transferred into comprehensible prose. The case being such, the instructor will oftentimes find it necessary to prescribe a procedure whereby advance preparation and rewriting will be required. One effective method used by many instructors is to require the preparation in advance of an outline and a rough copy of a composition. Then, during a class session the student finalizes the composition, turning in at the completion of the class the completed composition, the outline, and the rough draft. This method not only insures advance preparation and prewriting but also serves to discourage the student from turning in what is other than his own effort. Based upon the results of the evaluation of the theme, many instructors will also require another rewriting of the composition to correct errors or to effect improvement of certain aspects of the original composition.

The specimen papers which have been included in Exercise 31j provide the basis for meaningful student application to writing problems contained in compositions written by others. One effective method of critiquing these specimen papers is to divide the class into groups, have these groups discuss the papers, and then have members of these groups summarize group criticism before the class as a whole.

## Exercise 31c(1)

1. Vague. The phrases "gets out of college" and "depends on the college" are not specific enough to provide any meaningful guidance. A possible revision would be "A college which provides competent instruction, a wide variety of courses, and adequate library facilities offers a student the opportunity to get a good education."

2. Too general. The phrase "plays too large a role" is not sufficiently definitive to provide much real assistance to the composition writer. A possible revision would be "Government today, by providing favored tax status, discourages efficient business operations."

3. Vague. The fact that freshmen had not been able to select their courses in high school has no real causal relationship to what is happening in college. A possible revision would be "Freshmen ought to be allowed to select their own courses in college because, as mature persons, they realize what their curriculum goals are."

4. Too general. No positive guideline is provided concerning what students should do to make student government work. A possible revision would be "Student government can be an effective means of achieving student scholastic and social goals if students make their desires known to student government leaders and cooperate with them in attaining stated goals."

5. Vague. Some indication should be given in the thesis statement as to what "indiscriminate use" means and as to how such indiscriminate use can be stopped. A possible revision would be "Insecticides should be utilized only in accordance with specific regulations issued by government testing agencies."

6. Satisfactory, provided writer indicates specifically what he means by "limited," "undue weight" and "not enough weight."

7. Too general because it fails to indicate why mathematics should be required. A possible revision would be "Mathematics ought to be a required course for everyone because it requires disciplined thinking and provides the fundamental knowledge necessary to solve practical problems of a quantitative nature."

8. Satisfactory. However, the writer must specify his meaning of "educational" and "profitable."

9. Vague. A possible revision would be "A good teacher must possess knowledge of his subject, have the ability to communicate this knowledge, and have good rapport with his students."

10. Satisfactory.

11. Too general. The writer should tell us what the "interesting ideas" are.

12. Satisfactory, although the statement could be "tightened up" to read "The Book of Job is concerned with man's attempts to explain the existence of evil in a world created by a good God."

## Exercise 31e(1)

### FINDING A SUMMER JOB

I. Deciding on a job
   A. Consideration of camp jobs
   B. Review of part-time typing positions
   C. Considering child care
   D. Thinking about construction

II. Finding a job
   A. Studying the newspapers
   B. Visiting a placement service

III. Getting a job
   A. Arranging for interview
      1. By letter
      2. By phone
   B. Avoiding a bad impression
      1. By not appearing over-confident
      2. By not being self-deprecating
   C. Refusal of certain jobs
      1. Through rejection of uninteresting ones
      2. In rejection of ones too far from home

(III-C can also logically be outlined under II)

# THE VALUE OF PUBLIC OPINION POLLS

I. Operation of public opinion polls
   A. Selection of an important issue
   B. Scientific construction of questions
   C. Selection of population cross section
   D. Tabulation of replies
   E. Summary of results

II. Importance of polls in democratic process
   A. Revelation of public attitude
   B. Revelation of present groups' power
   C. Revelation of people's knowledge

# THE ADVANTAGES OF GOING TO COLLEGE

I. The advantages of classroom activities
   A. The values of liberal arts
      1. Gaining scientific knowledge
      2. Understanding literature
      3. Grasping a knowledge of social science
   B. The advantages of vocational training
      1. Understanding the educational processes
      2. Developing talents for a musical career
      3. Preparing to become an engineer

II. The opportunities of extracurricular activities
   A. The advantages of bull sessions
      1. Gaining understanding of subjects not
         discussed in class
      2. Improving in the art of discussing
   B. The values of sports
      1. Learning the spirit of competition
         a. Through indoor sports
         b. Through intercollegiate sports
      2. Developing physical prowess
         a. Through indoor sports
         b. Through outdoor sports

C. The benefits of social activities
   1. Associating with others
      a. Through clubs
      b. At dances
   2. Gaining new perspectives
      a. From speakers
      b. At concerts

## THE ADVANTAGES AND DISADVANTAGES OF A CITY UNIVERSITY

I. Advantages
  A. Transportation
  B. Hotels
  C. Stores
  D. Theaters
  E. Work opportunity
  F. Exposure to urban living
  G. Opportunity for greater independence

II. Disadvantages
  A. Many distractions
  B. Proximity to other schools

### Exercise 31f(2)

1. This beginning sentence catches the reader's interest with its humor, sets the tone of the essay, and introduces the subject of the essay effectively.

2. This statement, so unusual in a discussion of education, startles the reader and invites him to read on, to find out what is to be said for a bad education.

3. The humor of the opening sentence, both in its incongruity and its understatement, signals to the reader that this will be a less-than-scholarly discussion of the Civil War. The reader is also likely to wonder what it is that causes one to worry about the Civil War while changing a razor blade, and thus he will read on.

4.  Here again an unexpected assertion jars the reader's interest.

5.  The technique of kicking a sacred cow, which Mr. Ciardi employs here, is an effective way to arouse interest.

## SECTION 32

## EFFECTIVE PARAGRAPHS

The section on effective paragraphs provides discussion and exercises which can result in a profitable appraisal of paragraph unity, coherence, development, and consistency. Many instructors will want to go through Exercise 32(1) in class in the manner that the paragraph was approached in the initial part of Exercise 32. Such a procedure helps to provide a good overall initial understanding of unity, coherence, and development.

If the instructor has been utilizing outlining prior to the assignment of section 32a, a great deal will possibly already have been accomplished toward an understanding of unity. In section 32a, examples are provided which indicate the various ways in which topic sentences may be employed. It also brings out the fact that sometimes a topic sentence is implied. The following exercises, 32a(1-2) and 32b(1-2), provide a good basis for additional understanding of paragraph unity.

The ultimate test of good writing is coherence. This aspect of writing, more perhaps than any other aspect, requires the greatest amount of application in order that it be mastered. In sections 32c and 32d several good exercises have been provided which will provide training in the important aspects of proper chronological order, cause and effect relationship, consistent point of view, parallel grammatical structure, the repetition of key words and phrases to obtain coherence, and the effective use of transitional markers. All of these aspects are important--the one which is perhaps most helpful to students in achieving effective transition is the achievement in writing of a positive cause-effect relationship. If students can be assisted to achieve such a relationship in their writing, they will be well on their way to becoming effective writers.

Proper paragraph development is another extremely important aspect of writing. Section 32g provides several excellent illustrative paragraphs which instructors may want to discuss in some depth in class. Through such a process, students can be assisted to understand chronological order; use of spatial order; use of details, examples, and illustrations; analogy; comparison and contrast; repetition and restatement; definition; cause and effects; and elimination of alternatives. Each, of course, can be utilized to provide means of adequately developing material in a diversified manner. Exercises 32g(1-3) are three good application type exercises which should assist students in properly developing assigned subjects.

Consistency is another essential ingredient of good writing, and section 32 provides a number of paragraphs which are appropriate for class discussion in this respect. Additionally provided are specimen papers which can provide the means of discussing matters relative to the entire composition matters which have been discussed previously with respect to the paragraph. The "Whole Composition" review exercise on page 238 provides additional training in the preparation of a thesis statement, the sentence outline, and paragraph development. It is an exercise that many instructors will undoubtedly wish to take advantage of.

### Exercise 32(1)

1. Sentence 1 describes a situation which involves a general misunderstanding as to functions of certain editors. In combination with sentence 2, it indicates what these editors do or don't do. This sets the stage for a statement in sentence 3 as to actually what it is that the editors do. Sentence 4 shifts from third to first person plural and hence personalizes the writer's message. Sentence 4 also makes the reader aware how thoroughly he is at the mercy of such editors inasmuch as what is left is only what the editor wishes him to read. Having emphasized the general arbitrariness of the editor's action in sentences 5 and 6, the writer points out specific items of concern, introducing a new aspect--that of the reader's being confronted with something that has not only been condensed but is distorted. The effect of this deception upon the reader is described in sentence 7, leading up to the consequences of the deception in sentence 8, wherein he tries to discuss an abridged piece of writing that he has read with someone who has read the unabridged version.

The sentences in the first five sentences of this paragraph are tied together primarily through the use of pronouns. They in sentence 2 refers back to editors. They is used again in sentence 3 to refer to the previous sentence's subject. Then these editors ties sentence 4 to previous sentence. In sentence 5, in addition to the pronoun "we," which links the two sentences, "no idea what has been cut" refers in an obvious manner to actions of the editors, and sentence 6 deals with the results as a distortion. The consequent distortion becomes the linking point of discussion in sentences 7 and 8, the description changing from "distortion" in sentence 7 to "mutilated concept" in sentence 8.

2. Sentence 1 establishes a generalization relative to problems; and sentence 2, through the process of contrast, indicates in more specific terms what the difficult problems are as compared with problems in general. Sentences 3 and 4 provide details relative to the statement made in sentence 2 concerning the relationship of language to problems. Sentence 3 discusses such problems from the viewpoint of people in various positions. Sentence 4 lists specific instances involving reading, viewing, and speaking all of which require thinking. All of the activities also involve words, whether such words are spoken, written, or only thought. Sentence 5 concludes the paragraph with a reflection concerning the relationship between words and thoughts.

This conclusion, in effect, has been arrived at inductively. The sequence has gone from (1) general problems to (2) problems coming to our attention because of language to (3) problems which require words as a means to the solution to (4) specific items involving thinking, all of which can only be thought about by means of words spoken or visual. That there is a relationship between thoughts and words has been shown by adducing concrete examples; in the last sentence, though, the writer cannot go any further than to affirm such a relationship, since the exact nature of the relationship is still not known.

3. Sentence 1 establishes the generalization which becomes the topic sentence: "The late 1920's were an age of islands." In a general way, sentence 2 provides supporting detail. Further supporting the topic is sentence 3, in which the reader finds specific examples of both the real and the metaphorical islands. Further examples appear in sentence 4, which gives insight into the metaphorical islands as a means of hedonistic escape. Finally, sentence 5 summarizes earlier reflections--that people "everywhere," copying the ideas of others, are creating their own islands.

4. Sentence 1 presents in a highly uncomplimentary manner, the problem of man's "record of destruction" of his own world. Sentence 2, though somewhat general itself, presents two examples of such destruction: the shooting of shorebirds and the "near-extermination of egrets." Following the theme of man's destruction of life, sentence 3, the final sentence of the paragraph, catalogs classes of animals

affected by such destruction. It also specifies a new type of destruction: careless use of chemical insecticides. The final sentence not only supports the idea of man's ruthless conquest of nature, but it also refers to destructive chemicals—providing transitionally for a discussion which probably will come in the following paragraph.

5. In sentence 1 the reader is introduced to the topic of discussion: the Bogart the books celebrate based on a "handful of Warner movies." This Bogart looms considerably larger than Bogart, the man. Sentence 2 serves as supporting detail, indicating that the Bogart image was not established rapidly. Sentences 3 and 4 provide further support—first, that Bogart played numerous "minor roles"; and, second, that as a tennis player "in white flannels," he contrasted with the prim figure on film. Sentence 5 provides supporting details in specifying nine unsuccessful bids for a movie career, along with one successful film that set him on his way to fame. Sentence 6, though general, is highly effective in its brevity; it brings out the fact that a successful movie career is not necessarily stardom. Sentence 7 provides statistics in support of the general statement in the previous sentence. Sentence 8 indicates that his future was to be in tough guy roles. And, finally, sentence 9 summarizes the Bogart saga, reiterating that the Bogart image has resulted from his tough guy roles.

## Exercise 32a(1)

1. First sentence
2. First sentence
3. Combination of third and fourth sentences: "Today's bright and serious students are always putting administrators on the spot because they want to put the knowledge of the past to work in the present and to make the educational process provide a continuum between ideas and social and political action."
4. First sentence
5. Implied topic sentence: "Acceptance of the Negro revolt as part of the American myth assures that the revolt will continue."

## Exercise 32a(2)

1. Given my choice, I would sooner be in the Air Force than any other service branch. I am more interested in flying than in any other military occupation. Opportunities

for advancement are greater in the Air Force. Wages in certain brackets of the Air Force are higher than in other branches.

    2. The wreck on Route 64 at Mt. Nixon was caused entirely by carelessness and reckless driving by the driver of the Buick. When the wreck occurred the lights were green for the cars coming off the side road. A heavy truck loaded with hay was pulling out to cross the highway. The Buick came speeding down the main road, went through the stoplight, and crashed into the truck.

    3. We owe some of our notions of radar to scientific observations of bats. Scientists noticed that bats rarely collided with anything in their erratic flight. Keen eyesight could not be the reason for flying the way they do, since bats are blind. It was found that bats keep sending out noises inaudible to people and that they hear the echoes of those noises. This principle whereby they fly safely was found to be similar to the main principle of radar.

### Exercise 32b(1)

1. Sentences 4, 5, and 6.
2. Sentences 2 and 3. If sentence 2 is deleted, sentence 3, with the _so_ deleted, can follow sentence 1.
3. Sentence 5.
4. Sentences 5 and 6. However, if sentence 6 is made to follow sentence 1, and sentence 5 to follow sentence 1, all sentences will be relevant.
5. Sentences 4, 5, and 6.
6. Sentences 3 and 6.

### Exercise 32c(1)

    Thomas Hardy, English novelist, short story writer, and poet, is considered one of the most important of the writers who revolted against Victorian tradition at the end of the nineteenth century. A pessimist, he, in his more important novels--The Return of the Native, Tess of the D'Urbervilles, and Jude the Obscure--presented studies of life in the bleak English countryside, where individuals are defeated in their struggle against their physical and social environment and the caprices of chance. In 1928, he died at the age of eighty-eight.

Robert La Follette deserves the epithet "Fighting Bob."
In his college days at the University of Wisconsin, he became known as a debater and won an interstate contest.
After graduating from college, he worked for awhile in a law
office, but then, at twenty-five, he ran for district attorney of Madison County.  In spite of the opposition of the
regular Republican organization, he won as an independent
Republican.  But La Follette had higher ambitions.  After
serving one term as district attorney, he was elected to
Congress; after serving one term in Congress, he was elected
Governor of Wisconsin.  As a three-term governor, he continued to fight with words and ideas, and was successful in
initiating laws of direct primary, referendum, and recall.
The next step was the Senate, and again La Follette proved
his courage and independence by acting as spokesman for
small businessmen and farmers.  In 1924 he ran for President;
and although as a third-party candidate he had little chance
for victory, he did receive 4-1/2 million votes from
Americans who believed in "Fighting Bob" La Follette.


Exercise 32c(3)

1.  (3) Things move in cycles in sports, and a weak
team five years ago may be a champion now.  (1) Once upon a
time, before 1920, the whole American League hoped that by
some freak of fortune the weak New York Yankees might be
able to win a pennant.  (2) The mighty Red Sox and Athletics,
often tail-enders after 1920, were riding high.  (5) Even
the Browns, the last team to play a World's Series, were
very strong in 1922 and finally won the pennant in 1942.
(7) During the last eighteen years Detroit teams have ended
up in all eight positions.  (6) The standings are never the
same two years straight, and second division teams of last
year often are strong contenders this year.  (4) So let's
not lose interest in the home team; they may be up there
again soon.
2.  (7) Canasta became popular about 1950.  (1) There
were various reasons for the popularity of canasta.  (2) It
could be played by different numbers of players.  (3) Bridge,
of course, required no more and no less than four.  (5) Some
players found canasta more dramatic than bridge.  (6) They
liked the appeal of the different combinations of cards.
(8) Many card players liked the freedom of personal choice
and independence from a partner's decisions.  (4) Many people
naturally continued to like bridge.

3. (1) After World War II our leaders had various problems in framing our foreign policy. (6) Whether the wartime cooperation with the Russians could be continued, no one knew. (2) Few experts could be sure of the policy of the U.S.S.R. (5) The attitudes of the defeated Germans, Italians, and Japanese were uncertain. (3) The strength and the determination of our proven allies were questionable. (4) Seemingly no one anticipated developments in Indo-China and Korea. (7) The attitude of India and Pakistan on future developments was hard to determine.

### Exercise 32d(1)

Many students foolishly object to taking courses in writing. Their notion that only poets, novelists, and newspaper workers have to know how to write is unrealistic. While a student going into the technical or scientific fields may think that writing is something he seldom has to do, practicing engineers and scientists say they spend half their time writing letters and reports. Similarly, college students going into business think their secretaries will do their writing for them. Unfortunately, not only does this attitude show a naive faith in the competency of secretaries, but it fails to take into account the fact that young businessmen seldom have secretaries, competent or otherwise. Factors such as these would seem to suggest that, other things being equal, in any field a man who can express himself effectively is sure to succeed more rapidly than a man whose command of language is poor.

### Exercise 32d(2)

The United Nations is a potential source of world peace. It came into existence in 1945 after China, France, Great Britain, Russia, and the United States and a majority of other signing nations had ratified the Charter on October 24. One of the first peacekeeping tasks of the new organization was to investigate the border tensions and accusations between Arabs and Israelis in 1947. On two separate occasions since then the UN has made a truce, first in the Korean War, and later in the Indonesia-Netherlands dispute. More recently, UN troops have been active in the Congo, attempting to restore order since the Congo gained its independence from Belgium in 1960. In addition to active policing of peace, the UN, through the United Nations High Commissioner for Refugees, protects and helps refugees throughout the world by promoting international agreements on their legal status and by working with different governments for their admittance. The magnitude of the world refugee problem was emphasized in 1959, when seventy-four countries issued special stamps in support of the UN proclamation of a World Refugee Year. All of this, and much more, the UN has accomplished despite the fact that it is constantly in financial difficulty because some nations do not contribute sufficient funds to support it.

## Exercise 32d(3)

Radio amateurs, or hams, send messages on their home radio stations to people all over the world. Despite the fact that it takes a considerable amount of equipment to operate a ham radio, there are 260,000 licensed amateur stations in the United States. One of them is my cousin, Glenn Wade, who had D.R.T. as his signal code, which he used to broadcast as Dirty Rotten Tomatoes. There are four types of licenses hams may obtain from the FCC: (1) novice, (2) technician, (3) general class, and (4) extra class. Although their major purpose is recreation, the Federal Communications Commission has often praised these hams for their voluntary aid in times of emergency such as floods or storms.

## Exercise 32d(4)

1. Literature is a medium through which a person can convey his ideas towards or protests against different norms of society. A work that deals with a moral issue is of particular importance in literature; it is written with a particular purpose in mind. A literary work with a moral issue, such as a Shakespeare play, lives on to be reinterpreted by different generations. Such a work involves the reader, for he forms his own moral judgment towards the issue. Arthur Miller's Death of a Salesman is a play which deals with a moral issue.

2. It is difficult to feel compassion for a person who does not deserve it. My neighbor, John Carroll, is a poor little rich boy who just can't find happiness and love. He has never been deprived of anything except the one thing he really wanted, a girl who had gone to high school with him—a girl he couldn't get. His mother tells the story in such a way that it is easy to feel pity for this man because of this one thing that he couldn't attain. A person who least deserves compassion gets more than his share of it.

111

3. Every time a nation is involved in a war, it must face problems about its ex-soldiers after that war. Veterans are entitled to some special considerations from society, but treating them with complete fairness is a baffling problem. Livy reports that grants to former soldiers caused some troubles in the early history of Rome. There were many disagreements between them and the early Roman senators.

4. Preparing a surface for new paint is as important a step in the whole process as the application of the paint itself. First, be sure that the surface is quite clean. Wash any grease or grime from the woodwork. Use turpentine or a detergent for this. Be careful to clean off whatever cleanser is used. Then sand off any rough or chipped paint.

5. One of the books I read in high school English was Dickens' Tale of Two Cities. In it the author tells of some of the horrors of the French Revolution. He spends several pages telling about how the French aristocrats suffer. The climax of the book tells how a ne'er-do-well who had failed in life sacrifices himself for another. He takes his place in a prison and goes stoically to the guillotine for him.


## Exercise 32f(1)

Frederick Winslow Taylor was born in 1856. Fred's father was a lawyer. His mother was a cultured Easterner. She took the family abroad for three years. While at Exeter, Fred was a star baseball player and head of his class. He was short, heavily built, and sharp-tongued.

Fred began work as a machinist. He liked the men he worked with. He thought up new ways of doing things. When he became a foreman, he forgot about his working pals. He divided up jobs. In six years he became chief engineer. The idea of efficiently producing things went to his head. He lectured on production techniques at various colleges. Then he went to work for Bethlehem Steel. This job did not last long. The reason he lost his job was that he was more interested in production than in profit.

When he was thirty-four, he married. He began to play golf and entertain. He died in 1915 of pneumonia. He was one of the first efficiency experts.

The word <u>modern</u> has many meanings.  It may mean something new-fashioned or something characteristic of present or recent times  as modern painting, modern automobiles, or modern poetry.  To many people, particularly middle-aged or ancient adults, <u>modern</u> is a word of condemnation.  These people usually speak longingly of "the good old days," and anything modern is a "contraption," a device to make young people either sinful or lazy.  But to young people in general, <u>modern</u> is a word of high praise.  They use it to refer to things and ideas which are up to date, clever, speedy. However, I have little doubt that within twenty or thirty years these young-people-grown-old will be using the word just as their parents and grandparents use it now--as a word of condemnation.

## Exercise 32g(1)

1. Details, examples, and illustrations; comparison and contrast
2. Details, examples, and illustrations; comparison and contrast
3. Comparison and contrast; definition; illustration
4. Details, examples, and illustrations; repetition and restatement; explanation of causes and effects
5. Details, examples and illustrations; explanation of causes and effects
6. Chronological order; explanation of causes and effects
7. Chronological order; explanation of causes and effects
8. Spatial order; explanation of causes and effects
9. Comparison and contrast; illustration; causes and effects
10. Chronological order; details, examples, and illustrations; repetition and restatement
11. Repetition and restatement; explanation of causes and effects
12. Details, examples, and illustrations; comparison and contrast; explanation of causes and effects
13. Comparison and contrast; definition; examples and illustrations
14. Details, examples, and illustrations; definition
15. Comparison and contrast, explanation of causes and effects
16. Details, examples, and illustrations; comparison

and contrast; repetition and restatement
17. Explanation of causes and effects; illustrations and examples
18. Details, examples, and illustrations; comparison and contrast; explanation of causes and effects
19. Comparison and contrast; definition, explanation of causes and effects
20. Details, examples, and illustrations; comparison and contrast

## Exercise 32h(1)

1. Macleish's tone is dramatic and portentous. He used devices of parallel structure and antithesis and a striking allusion to Peter's betrayal of Christ to achieve a strong sense of urgency and a presentiment of disaster if what he proposes is not fulfilled. The aspect of a time of reckoning being near at hand is forcefully emphasized and re-emphasized by repeated assertion of failure to take positive action.

2. Krutch's tone is serious, contemplative, and touched with regret. After making several statements about man's nature ("It is not easy to live..."; "The faculty of wonder tires easily..."), he suggests in the last sentence the need for determination ("almost inevitably to have to try it") to achieve what, "alas," is so very difficult to achieve.

3. Mr. Gass' tone is informal and contains a strong recurring note of resignation which awards hysteria but which seems all the more ominous because of his matter of fact mode of presentation. He achieves an aspect of quiet despair by amassing a number of details tying in each observation to the color of hopelessness--gray. His final conclusion, that "everyone is out of luck who lives here," only serves by way of understatement to more poignantly accentuate the deplorable fate of those who live in the area he describes.

4. Churchill is addressing an audience that is certain of the rightness of the cause of freedom but wants to be inspired to heroic resistance. In the long series of parallel structures, the powerful repetition of "we shall fight," and the periodic final clause, we hear the strong voice of the representative man of freedom and the determined leader of a besieged nation.

5.  Typical of Faulkner's style, this passage suggests
both nostalgia for the fresh, exciting day of Ike's youth
and sorrow for the disappearance of the frontier. The
sentence structure attempts to recreate the thought process
of an old man remembering his youthful response to life.

## "Paragraph" Review Exercise

Specimen Paper 5 abounds in sweeping generalizations
and contradictory statements. In the first paragraph, for
example, the writer fails to take into consideration the
fact that while a university may exist primarily for its
students, that it has other legitimate purposes. Sentence
three contradicts sentence two in that if a university is a
substitute for parents, then students should not be expected
to make decisions for themselves. In effect, if the position is to be taken that students can make decisions for
themselves, then a redefinition of university function is in
order. Paragraph two attempts to establish a dichotomy between teaching and learning and ignores the basic premise
that teaching cannot take place unless learning is also
taking place. The last sentence in the paragraph is ambiguous; the writer apparently means that students should not
be required to take certain courses rather than that such
courses should be abolished. The third paragraph is awk-
wardly expressed and the first three sentences could better
be combined into one, such as: "It is time that the administration recognized that the students are best qualified to
evaluate professors because they are the only ones who can
best judge their effectiveness in the classroom." The last
paragraph concludes in an anticlimactic manner in that after
a belligerent, nonequivocal statement of student attitude, a
plea is entered for understanding.

Specimen Paper 6 deals too much in generalities and
lacks effective development. Its opening paragraph indicates that some positive details will be furnished which
will demonstrate how one can learn about life by working in
a department store. What follows, however, is more or less
a list of random observations but with no insight into what
made the people involved behave as they did. The transition
between the last two paragraphs is not effective; the but
indicates comments will be forthcoming contrary to what has
been said. Instead, the statement is made that the job was
rewarding and that it helped human relations—something that
would be expected from the previous context. The tone of
the last paragraph is lofty, but enough details have not

been provided to substantiate the conclusions which have been reached, and so the entire paper ends on an unconvincing note.

Specimen Paper 7 is generally well developed. In the first paragraph, the writer defines what he means by black nationalism and then supplies details to establish why the black identity was lost, something which provides an extra sense of urgency to the situation, and how the black is going about reestablishing that identity. The last paragraph ties in very nicely the reestablishment of identity phase with the importance of the past heritage. Had the writer not done this, he might have been criticized for spending too much time on history and not enough upon the reestablishment of identity aspect.

Specimen Paper 8 is cleverly written and the two examples it provides are developed in an interesting manner with an abundance of concrete details. The paper is an excellent example of inductive writing, wherein the author provides the substantiatory details first, making them provide a logical basis for the thesis that he adduces at the very end of the composition.

EFFECTIVE SENTENCES

In sections 33-36, sentence structure is approached from a rhetorical basis with the emphasis not so much upon the proper grammatical context as upon writing sentences to achieve definite effects. This, of course, is highly important in any writing, since the sentence is the basic structural element and unless versatility is employed in shaping sentences, the final compositional effort will lack verve and emphasis. What has the greatest effect upon the reader in expository writing is the logical development of thought. In close association with logical development is the way in which the sentences are tooled to effect a precision product, one in which various nuances of thought reflect an orderly process of development and a variety of presentation which makes what has been said interesting and coherent.

It has been said that the best type of writing is unobtrusive, that is, writing which provides a smooth roadway over which the writer's thoughts are transmitted in a seemingly effortless manner. In such an instance, the reader is often not conscious of the writing as such because it is accomplishing its basic mission, that of conveying the writer's message. In other words, the reader is not distracted by the writing; he is able to concentrate fully upon assimilating the content. His comment, then, as he reviews writing of this type will be with respect to the clarity, precision and directness of the development, all of which of course is really a tribute to the quality of the writing, since it has achieved the purpose of good expository writing--that of explaining clearly and persuasively.

The entire process can be likened to a glistening new automobile; the owner is conscious of the appearance and the performance; but unless he is mechanically inclined, he is not likely to be more than dimly aware of the functioning of hundreds of operating parts which contribute to the smoothness of operation. So it is with good writing; the reader appreciates the fact that information is clearly imparted but generally will not be concerned in determining how the overall effect has been produced. Were he to do so, he would find in large part that the writing has become what it is because of the way in which the sentences were construct-

ed.  He would find presentations of clear, smooth cause-
effect relationships;  skillful coordination and subordination; variety of sentence structure; the accurate and clear
utilization of connectives and sentences which vary in
length.  He would also discover parallel structure; sentence
thought arrangements leading up to an emphasis on main ideas
at the end of sentences; and a skillful use of active or
passive voice, depending upon what the writer has desired to
stress--the actor or the action.

In short, the good writer must be a good craftsman; and
unless he is a good craftsman with sentences, it is unlikely
that his overall writing effort will impress.  It is true
that it is the interaction of the parts which results in a
smooth functioning of the whole.  It is similarly true that
there is much more involved ultimately than just the sentences.  Nevertheless, unless the basic parts, in this case
the sentences, are skillfully fashioned to facilitate their
working together, the final effort is likely to sag.  It
could hardly be otherwise, since parts which in themselves
are improperly designed cannot ultimately be expected to
work together well.

SECTIONS 33-34

SUBORDINATION AND VARIETY

Section 33, which deals with the matter of subordination, contains several good exercises to assist the student to understand better this particular phase.  Sentence variety is covered in section 34, and exercises are provided to provide some training in revision of sentences to achieve better variety.  Exercises 34(1) and 34(2) are particularly good in assisting students to consider sentence variety in the paragraph context and in rewording sentences to achieve a particular style.

### Exercise 33

1.  Emphasis and unity in this sentence are achieved by subordination, positing a condition first followed by an anticipated result if that condition is allowed to continue to prevail. The sentence is coherent because <u>we</u> is the subject of both the dependent and independent clauses, and a strong relationship is implied with respect to a time comparison between past and present and the future.

2.  Maugham's sentence makes a general statement in the first independent clause. He then goes ahead in the rest of the sentence and substantiates that general statement by specifically indicating why the general statement is true. Something else, happiness, will sometimes provide the ennoblement the general statement concerns itself with, but suffering cannot because it results in a different effect upon character. The main emphasis in the sentence occurs at the end of the sentence wherein the consequences of suffering are depicted and coherence is maintained by repetition of the word <u>suffering</u> and the word <u>that</u>.

3.  The pronouns <u>they</u> and <u>this</u> assist in achieving coherence in this sentence.  After the initial general statement, a condition-result relationship forcefully establishes forcefully the lack of probability of exceptions to the general statement.  The main parts in the sentence, the general statement at the beginning and the independent clause at the end, are the parts at which emphasis is obtained.  The subordinate expression is in the middle.

4.  Sentence uses a colon to list and emphasize three aspects; _of these_ after the semicolon is the means by which the second part of the sentence relates back to the first. The placement of the verb and complement _is fever_ at the end of the sentence provides the means whereby the preceding phrases _by far the greatest_ and _by far the most terrible_ lead up to a climax culminating in _is fever_.

5.  Use of parallel structure gives coordinate emphasis to principal parts of sentence. The sentence is unusual in that the phrasing of the first and second parts are the same except for change of subjects and, in the case of the second part, for the word _not_ which provides the sharp contrast in meaning the author was striving for.

6.  This sentence has the subordinate clause after the independent clause with _they_ in the subordinate clause providing coherence between the two clauses to _eternal truth_. The effect of placing the subordinate clause last serves to emphasize what it takes for truths to become true or eternal rather than to emphasize the nature of eternal truths as such.

7.  The first part of the sentence is a clever parody of the famous line by Alexander Pope: "The proper study of mankind is man." The phrase following the coordinating conjunction _and_ establishes through the pronoun _it_ the timelessness of the activity being dealt with, and sets the stage for the pithy comment contained in the independent clause, at the end of the sentence.

8.  This sentence relies upon parallel structure and repetition of the word _love_ with the following prepositional phrases to achieve unity and coherence. Emphasis is achieved by the contrasting definition of _love of power_ in the second independent clause with the definition of _love of liberty_ in the first independent clause.

9.  The independent clause, which comes first, involves an imaginative personification, and the effect of the following subordinate clause is to render highly ludicrous the picture of certain types of statesmen and philosophers and divines, in that order, admiring something that inwardly is of the nature of a mischievous, irresponsible elf.

10. The imaginative comparison between a book and a mirror is very picturesquely supplemented by the further comparison

between individuals at two extremes--an ass and an apostle. The resulting commentary is a pithy one. For coherence purposes, various parts of the sentence are tied together by the words <u>peers</u>, <u>it</u>, and <u>look out</u>. The contrast between the blandness of the opening statement and the forcefulness of the following one, because of the strong contrast involved, heighten the effectiveness of the overall statement.


## Exercise 33a-d

1. The fate of the Concorde SST appears very grim; consequently, many airlines have decided not to buy the supersonic plane.

2. Ecological deterioration, over population, and natural resource depletion are serious problems; nevertheless, we are spending billions of dollars on new weapons of destruction.

3. Although society has changed radically during the past fifty years, most children still grow up to live the same kind lives their parents did.

4. Since there is a close relationship between vocabulary and success, students should try to improve their vocabularies.

5. Although daily exercise is useful for people of all ages, people over forty should not attempt to shovel snow unless they are in top physical condition.

6. Because the town was lax in its collection of taxes, the sanitation department was unable to collect garbage frequently enough.

7. Because biologists are concerned with finding new sources of food for the ever-growing world population, they are studying better methods of farming the ocean's fish and plant life.

8. The laser creates such a powerful ray that scientists find that it can accommodate twenty television channels or 20,000 telephone circuits.

9. Sentence is all right as originally written.

10. I enjoy spectator sports such as baseball, football, and hockey.

## Exercise 33e

1. Because he spent a great deal of time preparing for the exam, he got an "A" for the course.

2. He decided to vote for the incumbent after he learned that the other candidate was a bigot.

3. Because he said, "who so would be a man must be a nonconformist," Ralph Waldo Emerson was an individualist.

4. After the peace treaty was signed at noon, the prisoners knew that they would be free to come home at last.

5. Sentence is all right as it is given.

6. By pulling the emergency cord, she averted a train wreck.

7. Sentence is all right as originally written.

8. Although she was trying to economize, because she was already late for her dental appointment, she decided to take a taxi.

9. According to the popular ballad, although Casey Jones attempted to arrive on schedule, he was prevented from doing so by a head-on collision with another train.

10. William H. Vanderbilt once said, "The public be damned," a statement that indicated the attitude which characterized the maneuvers that made his father Cornelius and himself rich.

## Exercise 33f

1. With dawn breaking and the birds singing, it suddenly was good to be alive.

2. Although I tried my best, I flunked the course, and now I'll have to take it over again.

3. When I discovered that the bookshelves were too expensive, I went to the lumber yard and bought several shelves with brackets to hold them.

4. Sentence is good as originally written.

5. Because of the heavy traffic, we thought we might move faster on one of the side roads and so we tried to turn off the highway. / The traffic was heavy. Thinking we might move faster on one of the side roads, we tried to turn off the highway.

6. Since the whole family liked to go camping and any kind of travel would be cheaper with a trailer, they bought one.

7. When the new library was finished so was the money, and there were no books to put on the shelves.

8. When some skindivers went to an island off the Bahamas on an outing, sharks attacked them, one member of the group suffering severe lacerations of the right leg.

9. Because the professor talked too fast as he lectured, the students found it difficult to take notes.

10. When he came back, having served in the Peace Corps for two years, he decided to go back to school and qualify for a master's degree in social work.

## Exercise 33g

1. Having traveled through Eastern Europe, he decided also that he would apply for a visa to visit Yugoslavia although he had only a week left before he would have to report to work.

2. Bobby Fischer, who was universally regarded as a chess genius, was now ready to challenge the world champion, Boris Spassky. After some delays, the match was held in Reykjavik, Iceland.

3. Five hundred of the demonstrators, having been refused a permit for the march, gathered in the park and greeted the speeches of their leaders with applause.

4. Anthony Burgess' <u>A Clockwork Orange</u>, a best seller for many months, was made into a motion picture, directed by Stanley Kubrick, which was well-received by film critics.

5. First CBS, NBC, ABC and other television announcements of returns indicated that Richard Nixon, former vice-

president of the United States, who had narrowly been defeated by John F. Kennedy in 1960, had been elected President of The United States.

6. Having little time and less energy, I decided that my desk would have to remain in its untidy state.

7. The reporters flocked to the launch site, where the technicians were giving a last check to the spaceship that was to carry the three astronauts to the moon.

8. Muhammed Ali, who was known as Cassius Clay when he was heavyweight champion of the world, said he would resist induction into military service on the ground that he was an ordained minister of the Muslims.

9. My sports car, which has developed a rumble in the engine, worries me, since I can't repair it and I haven't the money to go to a mechanic.

10. Some psychiatrists have discovered that television is especially harmful to young children between the ages of three and five because it leads these children to equate violence with "good" men and acceptable behavior.

## Exercise 33h

1. She decided to take Route 91 to New York because she had taken it once before.

2. My parents bought a new house although they still liked the old one.

3. Although it was very cold, I continued to study.

4. President Nixon did not know in 1964 whether he ever wanted to run for office again.

5. I won a National Merit Scholarship; consequently I was very proud.

6. Because my best friends lived in New York, we would meet during vacations at my Uncle's.

7. I don't know whether I could paint, since I have never tried.

8.  I really don't feel that I should take the risk of
    going out in this weather -- not with the cold I have.

9.  Because she was dead tired, she lay down to rest.

10. Because the furnace broke down, the manager closed
    the office. / When the furnace broke down, the
    manager closed the office.


## Exercise 34a

1.  She decided to take the subway although she didn't
know the way and had to ask directions. The train agent was
very helpful.
2.  Because he had never smoked marijuana before, when
he was invited to a pot party, he went. Someone offered him
a "reefer," which he took. But since the effect was not
quite what he had expected, he didn't finish it. Instead,
he left the party.
3.  Joe DiMaggio was a great baseball player who could
hit, field, and run. Even more important, he had style.
4.  Because she wanted to go on the stage, she took
acting lessons and dancing lessons, practiced long hours,
and waited for her big opportunity. Finally it came.
5.  Hemingway perfected a unique style. He wrote in
short, very short sentences, sentences which could almost be
called "terse." This gave his stories an intense quality.
6.  Late-night TV talk shows are very popular. The
host is usually very funny. The guests are from many walks
of life. Because some of them are politicians and some are
show-business celebrities, they talk about various things.
The mixture makes for interesting conversation.
7.  TV documentaries, which are very interesting, have
shown the plight of the migrant workers, conditions in the
ghetto, and the helplessness of our neglected senior citizens. The one I like best is entitled "Birth and Death."
8.  The candidate smiled at the reporters, smoothed his
hair, fumbled in his pockets, and adjusted his glasses. He
was obviously stalling for time. Finally he cleared his
throat and began to speak.
9.  As the result of having served in Vietnam, he was
tired and sad. He had seen the face of war and the nature
of suffering. He hoped he would never have to see either
again.
10. I studied hard. I read the textbook, read outside
sources, and wrote a 15-page paper. I even bought the
instructor a Christmas present, but I flunked the course.

1. <u>Funny Girl</u>, which broke many box-office records during its long run on Broadway, was made into a movie starring Barbra Streisand.

2. The Olympics were held in Munich, Germany, in 1972. The United States won many gold medals, especially in swimming where Mark Spitz won seven. However, the murder of the Israeli athletes made many wonder whether there would be another Olympics.

3. Private colleges and universities throughout the country are in dire economic straits. Although many congressmen wish to provide such institutions with Federal funds, some of them may have to close their doors.

4. Women hold very important offices in other countries. However, in the United States, there is not a single woman senator. Although it is time for women to become more active politically, unfortunately many women are apathetic.

5. By giving bilingual education to children who have come to The United States from Cuba, Mexico, and Puerto Rico, they do not forget their heritage. However, leaders of Spanish-speaking communities believe that much still remains to be done.

6. I have a very small collection of records but I can't buy anymore, at least for the present, because I forgot and spent all the money I received as a Christmas gift on a new speaker for the stereo which I bought last year at a sale.

7. Several universities are becoming increasingly concerned over the young mothers who have been unable to contribute much to our society because they have been out of their fields while raising children. As a result, the universities have been providing grants so they can do post-graduate work and catch up.

8. The halfback was the star of the team. After running the kickoff back for a touchdown, he recovered a fumble and on the next play passed thirty yards for a second touchdown. By this time, particularly

after he had also kicked the extra point, he won the crowd's wild approval.

9. Although he was very interested in politics and had joined his campus chapter of the Young Republicans, he was almost certain that he preferred teaching as a career.

10. After dropping out of high school, he decided to get a job. When he couldn't find one, he decided to go back to school. Later he went on to college.


## Exercise 34c

1. Since the Surgeon General has determined that cigarette smoking is dangerous to your health, that warning is printed on every package of cigarettes. / Heed the Surgeon General's printed warning on every package of cigarettes that cigarette smoking is dangerous to your health.

2. Did John Lindsay's poor showing in the presidential primaries result in his deciding to quit the race? / Because John Lindsay did poorly in the presidential primaries, he decided to quit the race. / A decision to quit the race was the result of John Lindsay's poor showing in the presidential primaries.

3. There was much loss of life and devastation in the villages and cities of Nicaragua because of the earthquake, as the result of which The United States quickly offered assistance. / Because the earthquake caused much loss of life and devastation in the villages and cities of Nicaragua, The United States quickly offered assistance. / The causing of much loss of life and devastation in the villages and cities of Nicaragua by the earthquake resulted in The United States quickly offering assistance.

4. Devaluing the dollar made it more expensive to travel in Europe. / What will be the effect of devaluing the dollar? It will make it more expensive to travel in Europe. / Because the dollar was devalued, it was more expensive to travel in Europe.

5. Of the important contributions to American literature by black writers for more than a hundred and fifty

years, many educated people are still not aware./ Are
many educated people aware that black writers have made
important contributions to American literature for more
than a hundred and fifty years? No, they are not./
Although many black writers have made important contributions to American literature for more than a hundred
and fifty years, many educated people are still not
aware of it.

6. His head aching and his mouth feeling dry, he knew his
   hangover had begun./ There was an ache in his head and
   a dryness in his mouth; he knew his hangover had begun.
   / Because his head ached and his mouth felt dry, he
   knew his hangover had begun.

7. To dance is what they wanted to do, but the record
   player was broken./ Although they wanted to dance,
   the record player was broken./ Desiring to dance,
   they found that the record player was broken.

8. As they read <u>Catcher in the Rye</u>, high school students
   recognize in its hero a little of themselves./ In
   <u>Catcher in the Rye</u>, high school students recognize
   the hero as involving a little of themselves./ Reading
   <u>Catcher in the Rye</u>, high school students recognize
   in its hero a little of themselves.

9. Buying only old furniture and refinishing it
   themselves enabled them to furnish their new home at
   relatively little cost./ By buying only old furniture
   and refinishing it themselves, they furnished their
   new home at relatively little cost./ Since they bought
   only old furniture and refinished it themselves, they
   were able to furnish their new home at relatively
   little cost.

10. The institution of liberal reforms by Czechoslovakia
    led to its being invaded by Warsaw Pact countries./
    Did Czechoslovakia's institution of some liberal
    reforms lead to its invasion by Warsaw Pact countries?
    / Because it had instituted some liberal reforms,
    Czechoslovakia was invaded by Warsaw Pact countries.

Exercise 34(1)

The following is, of course, only one of many possible
rewritings.

As he slammed the front door, Mark felt better. He did not even glance over his shoulder to see if his parents were watching him. After walking to a nearby park, he sat down on the bench. Why his parents had yelled at him he knew very well. And he didn't blame them. They had both worked hard at their restaurant to keep him in comfort. They wanted him to have the opportunities that they had missed. They wanted him to become a doctor. But he couldn't seem to concentrate at school. Although he liked most of his teachers, he didn't really hear them, and just wanted to sleep in class. There was no denying that the marks he brought home were very poor. But he didn't want to be a doctor; he wanted to work with automobiles. The smell of gasoline, the sound of the motor, the shine of the chrome--those were the things that fascinated him. Tell them the truth, he thought. How can I be something I don't want to be? But he delayed returning home. He did not look forward to the scene they would make and the lack of understanding they would show.

## PARALLELISM

Section 35 covers one of the most important writing devices that can be utilized to achieve clear, direct, forceful, to the point sentences--parallelism. Many instructors who will want to emphasize parallelism will find the exercises in section 35 helpful for this purpose. One of the most famous of all books--the Holy Bible--fairly redounds with parallel structure; and classes are often intrigued when the instructor discusses certain passages from the Bible illustrating as he does how parallel structure assists the writers of the Bible in achieving the powerful, hammering effect so characteristic of this great work. There are so many good passages in the Bible to illustrate this particular effect that it is rather presumptuous to recommend any particular one. Nevertheless, many students have found the Book of Ecclesiastes to be particularly fascinating, and the first chapter of Ecclesiastes is an extremely appealing one. A consideration of such lines as "The sun also ariseth, and the sun goeth down and hasteth to the place where he arose" and "The thing that hath been, it is that which shall be: and that which is done is that which shall be done"; and "there is no new thing under the sun" offer all sorts of opportunities for a fruitful discussion as to how parallel structure assists the "gentle skeptic" in achieving his wistful, memorable account of the futility of all things mortal.

### Exercise 35a

1. The biography of Stillwell is an interesting, lively, and informative piece of writing.

2. Being too early, even if it wastes valuable time, is better than arriving late.

3. Mary has a full-time job, is a member of the school committee, and does her own housework.

4. Smoking cigarettes may be almost as dangerous as playing Russian roulette.

5. The popularity of marijuana comes partly from the fact that it is forbidden and partly from the fact that more young people want to escape reality.

6. The student was told to obtain a transcript of his grades and to apply for admission.

7. To be a good teacher, one must have patience, like to help others and show an infinite capacity for learning.

8. The policeman told us to drive very slowly and not to put on our bright lights.

9. The short story was powerful, shocking, and not easily understood.

10. Marcia moved to a new apartment with more space and with air-conditioning.

## Exercise 35b

1. He was both intelligent and courteous.

2. Sentence is correct as given.

3. The course not only is irrelevant, but the teacher also spends too much time talking about his hobbies.

4. The reviewer couldn't decide whether he should ignore the book or write an unfavorable review.

5. Hemingway was a good writer and influenced other writers.

6. A good politician not only works well with people but he also does not compromise his ideals.

7. She both had long hair and was very charming.

8. Neither was she beautiful nor did I find her clothes very tasteful.

9. Not only was Martin Luther King, Jr., an effective leader of men, but he also was an extremely good speaker.

10. The instructor both spoke slowly and a lot more loudly than was necessary.

Note that correction of the following requires attention to parallelism as well as to correlatives.

1. The press not only besieges the President, but also all members of Congress.

2. Either that's his wife or I'm mistaken.

3. He was both taller than and talked a lot more than I liked.

4. A good politician not only works well with people but he also does not compromise his ideals.

5. She both had long hair and was very charming.

6. Neither was she beautiful nor did I find her clothes very tasteful.

7. Not only was Martin Luther King, Jr., an effective leader of men, but he also was an extremely good speaker.

8. The instructor both spoke slowly and a lot more loudly than was necessary.

9. The snowplow operator was uncertain whether he should plow during the storm or wait until it was over.

10. Either this exam is too difficult or I didn't study enough.

## SECTION 36

### EMPHASIS

Section 36 involves exercises which stress emphasis
through placement of sentence elements, arrangement of sentence elements in proper order, repetition of sentence
elements, and use of active and passive voices. The "effective sentences" review exercise on page 269 provides a very
good test of student perceptiveness in identifying causes of
ineffective sentences and the rewording of such sentences to
provide increased power, vigor, and emphasis.

### Exercise 36a

1. In my opinion, he is an overbearing, egotistical
bore.
2. By and large, the results of the flood were disastrous.
3. As a rule, women are more perceptive and far more
sensitive than men are.
4. Tolstoy had, for the most part, a profound understanding of people and of the passions that drive them.
5. If I had my way, this university would be closed
and its faculty fired.
6. Teddy Roosevelt, I have read, was dynamic and full
of life.
7. Test results prove, in most cases, that smoking
seriously impairs the health.
8. It seems to me that the lawyer shirked his respon-
sibility and the judge was biased.
9. The day was clear, the sun was shining, and the
snow was packed hard; in my opinion, it was a great day for
skiing.
10. With its superior technology and its single-minded
determination, if everything goes right, the U.S. will
definitely win the space race.

### Exercise 36b

1. After her marriage broke up, she began seeing a
psychiatrist regularly.

2. After his first business failed, he started a new business and made a million dollars.

3. Although we tried to keep it in a cool place, the wine turned to vinegar.

4. The rowers bending rhythmically and the oars flashing in the sun, the boat neared the finish line.

5. Stamping their feet and blowing on their fingers, they stood the cold for an hour.

6. Several years ago on a three-lane highway in Minnesota, I saw two cars crash head-on.

7. After she suffered a severe depression, her doctor insisted that she take a vacation.

8. If, after you have finished typing it, the footnotes are in good order, your research paper will be accepted.

9. Although she had checked her figures and added again, Norma still had not balanced her accounts.

10. Between the ship and the shore lay three miles of rough water.

## Exercise 36c

1. He moved away from the city because he wanted to let his dog run, his rent was high, and he was ill.

2. Most students get bored with school after years of elementary school, high school, and college.

3. She inherited some jewelry, a house, and a million dollars.

4. The play received terrible reviews and closed after the first week.

5. The candidate smiled at the children, mingled with men in the street, and promised a guaranteed income for all.

6. Charles is a poker player, a capable gardener, and a

famous doctor, (If an anticlimax is intended,
sentence can be left as given.)

7. We find similar psychological reactions in frogs,
rats and guinea pigs to those of men.

8. During his vacation David acquired a bad sunburn,
some souvenirs, and a wife.  If an anticlimax is
intended, it might be written as follows:  David
acquired a wife, some souvenirs, and a bad sunburn.

9. The earthquake toppled several of the buildings in
the area and caused 100 deaths.

10. Laurence Olivier is a director and producer as well
as being one of the great Shakespearean actors of
all time.

## Exercise 36e

1. The architect remodeled the deserted warehouse as
an office building.

2. The press scrutinized police procedures.

3. The Senate will investigate the Watergate affair.

4. My parents planned an addition to the house.

5. The reporters interviewed the returned astronauts.

6. The chairman of the refreshments committee selected
the menu.

7. The administration severely criticized the release of
the Pentagon Papers.

8. Drunken drivers cause many major accidents.

9. The local Department of Health distributes polio
vaccine.

10. Vice President Agnew attacked television and the
press.

1. COOR - Henry Kissinger was formerly a professor at Harvard University.
2. SUB - Because the child was terrified and confused, he fell exhausted on the wet leaves.
3. SUB, COOR - Robert Frost, a poet, wrote about rural New England and the human condition.
4. PAR - After reading the book, Susan decided to change her way of life and her plans for the future.
5. SUB - Although the fighter was very strong and in excellent condition, he was knocked out in the fifth round.
6. EMP - It is a shame that poverty still exists in The United States because we are the wealthiest nation on earth, there is no excuse for it, and it's about time we eradicated it.
7. EMP - India and Pakistan are but two examples of the many countries suffering from overpopulation.
8. PAR - Some college students regard their education as irrelevant and not useful.
9. SUB - After working in the Peace Corps for two years and after refusing several job offers, Elizabeth returned to school.
10. PAR - He leaned back in his chair, closed his eyes, rested his hands on his lap, and went to sleep.
11. EMP - While Chekhov attended medical school, he write short stories to support his family.
12. SUB, PAR - The substitute teacher, a married woman with a good sense of humor, conveyed her ardent love of science to her classes.
13. PAR - To a naughty child, a scolding parent seems like a giant standing seven feet tall with a large mouth and eyes that glare in the dark.
14. SUB - Not only our love of Colonial arts and crafts but also our love of modern technological skills is reflected in our homes and magazines.
15. SUB - In Arizona, the state with the largest Indian population, live the Hopi, Navajo, and Apache.
16. PAR - To become a responsible voter you should know the issues, listen to the candidates, become familiar with their views, learn their weaknesses, and come to know their strengths. Then you can make a wise choice.
17. SUB - When Rachel Carson wrote a great deal about the

dangers of insecticides, she was vigorously opposed
by insecticide companies and by people who find
insecticides helpful.  But what about the people
who have been poisoned by them?

18. SUB - Harlem, which is infested with rats and disease,
is reached by walking up Fifth Avenue, the most
glamorous street in the richest city in the world.

19. EMP - A movie was made that recalled those days when
the Boston Strangler roamed free, and terror gripped
the city of Boston.

20. SUB - One reason that the space trip was an
unqualified success was that the astronauts had been
kept in seclusion for weeks before it to guard them
against infection.

# SECTION 37

## LOGIC

Logical thinking is essential to all types of writing and, in effect, the first composition a student writes should be, if it is a good one, one which is logically organized. For this reason a good case can be made for dealing with the material in section 37 at an early stage of the course. On the other hand, even though logic is initially important it is equally true that the other aspects of composition are also important at the time of the first writing assignment. So, since not everything relating to composition can be covered comprehensively at one time, some arbitrary order of selection is going to have to be made. Accordingly, many instructors may decide that although logic is important at any stage of the course, it should be emphasized as a course unit of its own after some of the less difficult aspects have been covered. As a matter of fact, many freshman composition courses are structured to take up argumentative writing in the second term of the course; where this is true, the tendency often will be to reserve a detailed treatment of logic until the time that argument is being covered.

Closely related to the logical process is the matter of definition. Section 37a contains a discussion of informal and formal definitions with additional clarification as to what is involved in an extended definition. Exercise 37a provides the basis for the examination of the validity of several statements which are offered as definitions.

The importance of avoiding hasty or broad generalizations is stressed by section 37b, with exercise 37b providing for the analysis of given generalizations. Restatements of sentences are required where generalizations are determined to be based on inadequate evidence.

Some of the more common fallacies are discussed in sections 37c and 37d. Particular emphasis is placed upon achieving a proper cause-effect relationship, something that many students do not manage to attain in their writing--with the result that their compositional efforts are unconvincing. Inability to establish clear cause-effect relationships in the development of an idea often results in writing which lacks transition and smoothness. Even worse are instances wherein wrong conclusions are drawn from statements in the compositional context. For this reason, many instructors may want to take such steps as are necessary to assure that students are thoroughly conversant with such fallacies as the post hoc, ergo propter hoc fallacy, the non-sequitur, begging the question, false analogies, and assumptions that only two alternatives exist when there are actually more than two possible. Exercise 37d involves an analysis of sentences to determine which rules of logic have been violated. Exercises 37(1) and 37(2) provide for the logical analysis of paragraphs and the "Logic" review exercise requires students to examine critically advertisements, newspapers, and magazines with the objective of having them ascertain for themselves instances wherein rules of logic have been violated by other writers.

## Exercise 37a

1. The meaning of "knowledge" and "skill" is not made clear, and "school" seems to be synonymous with "education." We do not know whether the writer is talking about the process of education, the purpose of education, or the result of education.

2. The definition lacks parallel form and fails to take into consideration the hitting of the ball and the scoring of a run.

3. The definition lacks parallel form. It also should express some of the actions of the participants as a result of the smoking of the marijuana.

4. The definition is a valid definition although examples would be required concerning the ways in which people are involved.

5. This is a definition by word substitution. The definition is not, however, expressed in a parallel form.

6. The definition given is a valid definition. It has a genus ("a swelling") and a differentiation (due to ... patella). It could be improved, particularly for a lay audience, by "swelling of the ..." and "caused by much kneeling."

7. The definition lacks parallel form. It could be better expressed as "Analysis is the breaking up of any whole ..." It also needs to be differentiated such as "for the purpose of determining, studying, etc."

8. What is involved is a definition by word substitution. However, the difference should be brought out between boeuf bourguignon as fancy beef stew and beef stew

generally.

9. The definition lacks parallel form and should be rewritten to avoid the use of "is when." It also should be extended to include acts not necessarily in violation of orders but which are intended to diminish the authority or detract from the success of the ruling authority.

10. The definition is acceptable only as a "poetic" definition but one which is, of course, valid (one might say necessary) in poetic context.

## Exercise 37b

1. This statement involves an overgeneralization. Lobbying has legal status as a legitimate activity. Certainly, lobbyists espouse special interests but the fact that they influence legislation does not mean that their activities as such or the result of their activities are dishonest.

2. Although many young people do not obey their parents either in all or in some respects, many others do. If this statement, consequently, is to be an accurate generalization, it should be prefaced by some or an equivalent restrictive term.

3. A statement such as this would require documentation to be acceptable.

4. The statement is exaggerated and should be reworded to something like "Many intelligent men find it impossible to believe in religion in the twentieth century."

5. Very probably, some women who support women's liberation are frustrated and unsuccessful. On the other hand, there are many who support the movement who cannot be placed in either of these categories. Consequently, the statement to be acceptable would have to be prefaced by some or an equivalent restrictive term.

6. "Many studies have shown that college graduates make more money on the average than noncollege graduates" would be a better way of stating this one.

7. This statement is obviously not always true. "A good book is usually an interesting book" would be better.

8. The statement is an exaggeration because of the use of the word _any_. A better generalization would be "Many intelligent people believe that birth control information should be disseminated by the government."

9. This statement is too sweeping to be acceptable. To corroborate such a statement, a definition of success would first have to be offered. Then, if evidence could be accumulated which indicates that more students qualify for the definition of success than those who do not, a revised, more restrictive statement to this effect might be acceptable.

10. A great deal of substantiating evidence would have to be offered to support such a broad generalization. Without such evidence, the statement can hardly be accepted as factual.

## Exercise 37c

1. Prejudgment. The fact that movie stars are good-looking is not in itself a reason for unsuccessful marriages. Investigation into many movie star marriages would have to be made before any valid conclusions could be reached as to whether such marriages are generally unhappy or the reasons therefor if the case were such.

2. Transfer. What is true of an individual is not necessarily true of the government which has financial resources available that an individual does not have. The statement under discussion also rests upon an analogy and could be developed into an argument from analogy.

3. Transfer. Attitudes of an ancient people are in many respects not the same as those of a modern people. Also, even where punishment is involved, modes of punishment vary greatly over the years.

4. Bandwagon. Politicians are sometimes held in low esteem and many people don't need much convincing that what politicians do is wrong.

5. Argumentum ad hominem. Although one may not approve of a person because he is an atheist, the fact that he is an atheist doesn't mean that he can't teach.

6. Transfer. The word _pampered_ has an undesirable connotation as far as many people are concerned and identifying college students as pampered children prejudices many people against them.

7. Argumentum ad hominem. The fact that the man was a criminal doesn't necessarily mean he is now criminally inclined.

8. Prejudgment based upon a hasty generalization.
What one Paris hotel did is not necessarily indicative of
what the French in general do.

9. Bandwagon. Many people believe black people to be
naturally rhythmic because of the great success of many
black musicians. However, many other blacks would have to
be considered before blacks in general could be so regarded.

10. Prejudgment and Argumentum ad hominem. Most people
don't like draft resisters, but the reason for some individuals resisting the draft may not be that they are afraid to
die for their country but, rather, that they question the
cause for which they might have to die were they to be
drafted.

## Exercise 37d

1. Begging the question
2. Post hoc
3. Non Sequitur
4. Non Sequitur
5. False analogy
6. Non Sequitur
7. Non Sequitur
8. Non Sequitur
9. Post hoc
10. Post hoc

In dealing with illogical statements one problem is
that all examples of fallacious reasoning are non sequiturs
in that their conclusions do not follow from their premises.
Begging the question may be an exception to this, but both
false analogy and post hoc fallacies are non sequiturs; thus
all of these, with the possible exception of the first, may
be accurately judged to be non sequiturs, though 5 is also
a false analogy and 2, 9, and 10 are also post hoc fallacies.

## Exercise 37(1)

Both speakers fail to develop a logical argument. Mr.
Jones uses charged language instead of clearly defined
terms. His generalizations are hasty and overstated, and
he concludes his remarks with a non sequitur. Mr. Smith
responds with a false analogy, an ad hominem, an overstated
generalization, a non sequitur and in effect does not deal
with the problem of the standards of literacy and journalism
Mr. Jones is concerned about.

142

The selection abounds with _argumentum_ _ad_ _hominems_. The first paragraph contains several vilificatory comments about sportswriters: "These tin-horn sports," "these semiliterate dealers in cliches," "misinformation and moronic opinions." The second paragraph attacks sportswriters as lacking objectivity and penetration. Several good examples are provided which indicate sportswriters' lack of penetration, but the writer offers no proof that sportswriters are not objective. Obviously the sportswriter has to tell who won and, in the last analysis, if a team won it must have played a better game at least as far as the final score is concerned. Stating that a team's supporters wanted to win is neither irrelevant nor vicious although it might be considered a self-evident fact.

More name-calling takes place in the third paragraph. There can be little doubt that a great deal of small talk takes place during the description of a football game and that many cliches are uttered such as "the game isn't over until the final gun sounds." But a football game is not staged with the idea of providing high level intellectual activity for the viewer. In the last analysis, the writer would have done better had he eschewed personal invective and concentrated upon some constructive criticism as to how the game could have been described more graphically for the viewer.

SECTIONS 38-44

WORDS

Many students have difficulties with diction, but for
various reasons.  Some have trouble expressing themselves
properly because of a limited vocabulary; some have an
adequate enough vocabulary but do not find it easy to put it
together smoothly; still others mistake pomposity and
elaborateness of structure for erudition, and put something
together that makes for very turgid, tiresome reading.

What to do, then, to achieve precision of expression becomes a matter of considerable effort; writing and rewriting
of compositions would seem to be an essential part of the
corrective process.  At the same time, assignment and discussion of specific exercises to sharpen aspects of diction
is oftentimes of considerable benefit as well.

The Prentice-Hall Handbook for Writers has several good
exercises concerning utilization of the dictionary.  If
properly used, they can be of considerable benefit to the
student.  The key to the situation, of course, is whether
or not the dictionary is being properly used; and, in most
instances, if the student is not required to participate in
a meaningful dictionary unit, it will not be.  On the other
hand, class assignments which require a student to explore
and utilize a dictionary comprehensively can often help
convince the student of the dictionary's utility.

Precision of expression can be achieved only if one is
aware of the connotative as well as the denotative meanings
of words.  Many students are not aware that synonyms do not
mean exactly the same thing.  A little dictionary work with
synonyms will often help to develop an awareness of the
precise meanings of words.  Approximate homonyms as they are
discussed in section 40c represent an area which causes a
great deal of confusion in written communication.  Many
instructors will want to make students aware of some face-
reddening errors that can result such as when one "eludes"
to something rather than "alludes" to it, or when one speaks
of a couple having "martial" difficulties rather than
"marital" difficulties.

Since many students will tend to write too informally, a discussion and an exercise or two on slang and substandard English as provided by the text may help to overcome this difficulty. For those who harbor the illusion that quantities of words and involved expressions are emblematic of intellectuality, some of the exercises in section 41 may be helpful.

Spelling is an area which usually offers considerable challenge to many college students. While it is true that spelling is an elementary school subject, it is one elementary school subject that has not been too well mastered. In the college classroom, then, the instructor is placed in a dilemma. On the one hand, the position can be taken that a college composition class should not have to spend time on such an elementary subject; on the other hand, if frequent misspellings are encountered, such deficiencies can hardly be ignored. Section 44 discusses a few of the time-tested rules which have helped many students with spelling difficulties; some meaningful exercises are also provided which provide for work in areas that are particularly troublesome. Section 44g provides spelling lists of many troublesome words which instructors may desire to commend to the attention of particular students.

SECTION 38

THE DICTIONARY

Few will deny the importance of the dictionary to the
student.  Too often, however, the dictionary ends up somewhat like Mark Twain's weather--everybody talks about it,
but nobody does anything about it.  The result is that many
students get all the way through high school and college
with no more than a nodding acquaintance with a work which
could benefit them greatly--if they knew how to use it.

What to do about it, then, is the problem.  Section 38
provides an extensive basis for instructors who would like
to establish a dictionary unit; other instructors who desire
to spend a limited amount of time on the dictionary may want
to use only some of its exercises.  Many instructors have
found it profitable to require students to compare several
desk dictionaries from the viewpoint of such aspects as
pronunciation, etymology, clarity of meaning, synonymies,
nature of grammatical treatment, and labels.  Such a comparison can be made relative to the sample word howl
discussed on pp. 287-292 in section 38 or, if reproductive
facilities are available, by distributing copies of pages
from various dictionaries which deal as much as possible
with the same range of words.

Still another way is to prepare handout sheets which
will provide complete dictionary entries of four or five
words from four or five of the best desk dictionaries.
Utilizing the handout sheets selected students can be asked
to indicate differences between the dictionaries, and to
express opinions as to the respects in which certain of the
dictionaries surpass the others.  These comments, in turn,
can be made the basis for a composition with such titles as
"The Best Standard Desk Dictionary," "The Characteristics
of a Good Desk Dictionary," "What I Like About the New World
Dictionary," "A Comparison of Etymological Development in
the Most Widely Used Standard Desk Dictionaries," and many
other similar subjects.  Writing a composition about dictionaries based upon a study of dictionaries has the advantage
of imposing a unified, overall approach to the subject--one
which requires the student to perform some basic research
prior to the time he writes.  As such, then, it satisfies a
dual function.  It gives the student something to write

about and it provides a meaningful approach whereby the student can learn a great deal about the dictionary.

Section 38 provides several other good exercises which will require students to explore thoroughly what their own desk dictionaries have to offer. Such exercises provide a variety of fact-finding activities involving such aspects as preferred spelling of words (some students will be surprised to learn from Exercise 38(1) that sometimes more than one spelling is possible for certain words); hyphenization or nonhyphenization of certain words (Exercise 38(2)), and information, Exercise 38(3), as to whether such foreign terms as <u>bon voyage</u> are regarded as naturalized terms and hence no longer require italicizing. Exercises 38(4) and Exercise 38(5) provide for dictionary use to determine word pronunciations and Exercise 38(6-8) involves work relative to etymologies. Still additional exercises provide for student utilization of dictionaries to ascertain word meanings, grammatical information, and usage labels. The last exercise, Exercise 38(17), requires the student to utilize various dictionary sections, including appendices, to determine answers to certain questions.

### Exercise 38(1)

In this and subsequent dictionary exercises some variation may be expected since the four major desk dictionaries show minor variations. Where answers provided are based on a single dictionary, that dictionary is indicated in parentheses after the page and exercise number.

Where alternatives are listed for the items in these exercises they are found without qualification in one or more of the four dictionaries suggested.

| or esthetic | demon | licorice |
| catalog | or inclose | or modelled |
| catsup | favor | Shakespeare |
| criticize | judgment | theater |

| | | |
|---|---|---|
| bookshop | jazzmen | supermarket |
| castoff | passkey | up-to-date |
| easygoing | self-government | well marked |
| houseboat | showdown | worldwide |

## Exercise 38(3)

Note that dictionaries vary widely in this matter. Webster's 7th considers it too subjective a matter to be prescribed.

| | | |
|---|---|---|
| <u>bon voyage</u> | <u>dramatis personae</u> | resume |
| <u>coup d'etat</u> | matinee (or matinee) | <u>sine qua non</u> |
| creche | <u>nouveau riche</u> | Weltschmertz |
| debutante | | |

## Exercise 38(4)

| | |
|---|---|
| ə dult', ad'ult | eks'kwi-zit, ik. skwiz'it |
| ā'lē əs, al'yəs | for' mi. də. bəl |
| ser' ə brəl, səre' brəl | jen' yōō. in |
| des' pik əb'l, di spik'əb'l | grē' sē, grē' zē |
| | im' pə tənt |
| | mis' chi. vəs |
| | ri surch', rē' surch |
| | root, rout |

## Exercise 38(5)

1. French; Medieval Latin <u>assassinus</u>; Arabic hashshāshĭn, hashis eaters < <u>hashĭsh</u>, hemp.

2. Middle English <u>Bedlem</u>, <u>Bethlem</u> $<$ the London hospital of St. Mary of Bethlehem.

3. Blend of <u>drag</u> and drabble.

4. Middle English <u>egg</u>, <u>egge</u> $<$ Old Norse <u>egg</u> $<$ Anglo-Saxon <u>aeg</u> (probable Indo-European base *<u>owjom</u>-, *<u>ojom</u>, laid by a bird).

5. Middle English and Old French <u>familier</u>; Latin <u>familiaris</u>, of a household, domestic $<$ <u>familia</u>.

6. French; fedora (1882), play by Sardom.

7. Medieval Latin <u>incisivus</u> $<$ Latin <u>incisus</u>, past participle of <u>incidere</u>, to cut into $<$ <u>in-</u>, into + <u>caedere</u>, to cut.

8. French; <u>lampon</u> $<$ <u>lampons</u>, let us drink -- refrain in a drinking song $<$ <u>lamper</u>, to drink

9. Middle English <u>neighbour</u>, nyebour; Anglo-Saxon <u>neaghbur</u> $<$ <u>neah</u>, <u>nigh</u> (basic sense, "turned toward, looking toward") + <u>gebur</u>, freeholder, peasant, farmer.

10. ME, <u>organizacion</u> $<$ ML, <u>organizatio</u>.

11. Middle English <u>prest</u>, <u>preost</u>; Anglo-Saxon <u>preast</u> $<$ Late Latin <u>presbyter</u>, an elder; Greek <u>presbyteros</u>, elder, comparative of <u>presbys</u>, old, an old man. (cf. Sanskrit <u>purugava</u>, a guide, leader, originally of a herd of oxen.)

12. After John Montagu, 4th Earl of <u>Sandwich</u> (1718-1792), said to have eaten these in order not to leave the gaming table for meals.

13. Middle English <u>schirte</u>, <u>schurte</u>; Anglo-Saxon <u>scyrte</u> $<$ *skurti $<$ base of <u>scort</u>, shert; akin to German <u>schurze</u>, apron, doublet of English <u>skirt</u>; basic sense "short garment."

14. Middle English; Old Norse <u>skyrt</u>, shirt, <u>kirtle</u>, exactly cognate with Anglo-Saxon <u>scyrte</u>. (See <u>shirt</u> above.)

15. Gaelic <u>sluggh-ghairn</u> $<$ <u>sluagh,</u> a host + <u>gairm</u>, a call.

16. $<$ earlier <u>quelch</u> (fusion of <u>quell</u> and <u>crush</u>) with
    <u>s</u>- intensifier.

## Exercise 38(6)

1.  André Marie Ampère, French physicist and mathematician.

2.  Captain Boycott, land agent ostracized by his
    neighbors during the Land League agitation in Ireland
    in 1880.

3.  Nicolas Chauvin, soldier of Napoleon I, notorious
    for his bellicose attachment to the lost imperial
    cause.

4.  Johns Duns Scotus, called the "Subtle Doctor" (died
    c. 1308) whose followers, called <u>Dunsmen</u>, <u>Duncemen</u>
    and Renaissance humanism;  the word came to be
    applied to any opponent of education, and then to
    a stupid person.

5.  Alexander Gorden (1730-1791), American botanist.

6.  John L. MacAdam (1756-1836), Scottish engineer who
    invented the process.

7.  Vidkun Quisling (1887-1945), Norwegian politician
    who betrayed his country and became its puppet ruler.

8.  General H. Shrapnel (1761-1842), of the British Army,
    who invented it.

9.  Ulster, Ireland, where originally made and worn.

10. James Watt (1736-1819), Scottish inventor.

## Exercise 38(7)

1.  almanac - Arabic

2.  cherub - Hebrew

3.  cockatoo - Malayan

4.  dory - American Indian (Central America)

5.  goulash - Hungarian

6. huckster - Middle English or Middle Dutch

7. jute - East Indian, Sanskrit

8. kerosene - Greek

9. moccasin - American Indian (Algonquian)

10. mukluk - Eskimo

11. piano - Italian

12. squadron - Italian

13. trek - South African Dutch

14. tulip - Turkish

15. typhoon - Chinese

## Exercise 38(8)

1. almanac - Arabic   2. cherub - Hebrew   3. cockatoo - Malayan   4. dory - American Indian (Central America) 5. goulash - Hungarian   6. huckster - Middle English or Middle Dutch   7. jute - East Indian, Sanskrit   8. kerosene - Greek   9. moccasin - American Indian (Algonquian) 10. mukluk - Eskimo   11. piano - Italian   12. squadron - Italian   13. trek - South African Dutch   14. tulip - Turkish   15. typhoon - Chinese

## Exercise 38(9)

Dictionaries vary widely in method of listing. The American College is followed here since it provides the most convenient listing.

call - 43                 land - 17                 run - 104 get – 20                     light – 64                      set – 67

go – 43                      out – 55                        turn – 93

high – 32

## Exercise 38(10) (Webster's 7th)

1. bounty – 1. liberality in giving: generosity; 2. something that is given generously; 3. yield esp. of a crop; 4. a reward, premium, or subsidy esp. when offered or given by a government: as (a) a grant to encourage an industry (b) a payment to encourage the destruction of noxious animals.
2. complexion – 1. the combination of the hot, cold, moist, and dry qualities held in medieval physiology to determine the quality of a body; 2. (a) an individual complex of ways of thinking or feeling; (b) a complex of attitudes and inclinations; 3. the hue or appearance of the skin and esp. of the face; 4. general appearance or impression.
3. engine – 1. obs. (a) ingenuity; (b) evil contrivance; wile; 2. archaic: something used to effect a purpose: agent; 3. (a) a mechanical tool: as (1) an instrument or machine of war (2) obs. a torture implement (b) Machinery (c) any of various mechanical appliances –– compare fire engine; 4. a machine for converting any of various forms of energy into mechanical force and motion; 5. a railroad locomotive.
4. fond – 1. foolish, silly (–– pride); 2. (a) prizing highly; desirous (–– of praise) (b) strongly attracted or predisposed (of music); 3. (a) foolishly tender; indulgent (a –– mother) (b) loving, affectionate (a –– wife); 4. doted on: dear (his ––est hopes).
5. generous – 1. archaic: highborn; 2. (a) characterized by a noble or forbearing spirit; magnanimous, kindly; (b) liberal in giving; openhanded; (c) marked by abundance or ample proportions; copious (d) full-flavored (–– wine).
6. gossip – 1. dial. Brit: godparent; (b) companion, crony; (c) a person who habitually reveals personal or sensational facts; 2. (a) rumor or report of an intimate nature; (b) a chatty talk.
7. humor – 1. (a) a normal functioning fluid or semifluid of the body; (b) a secretion that is an excitant of activity; 2. (a) in medieval physiology; a fluid or juice of an animal or plant: specif: one of the four

fluids entering into the constitution of the body and determining by their relative proportions a person's health and temperament; (b) habit, temperament; (c) temporary state of mind; (d) a sudden, unpredictable, or unreasoning inclination: whim; 3. (a) that quality which appeals to a sense of the ludicrous or absurdly incongruous; (b) the mental faculty of discovering, expressing, or appreciating the ludicrous or absurdly incongruous; (c) something that is or is designed to be comical or amusing.

8. intern - 1. adj. archaic (a) internal; 2. to confine or impound esp. during a war; 3. intern or interne: an advanced student or graduate esp. in medicine gaining supervised practical experience (as in a hospital).

9. knave - 1. archaic (a) a boy servant; (b) a male servant; (c) a man of humble birth or position; 2. a tricky deceitful fellow; rogue, rascal; 3. Jack: a playing card carrying the figure of a soldier or servant and ranking usually below the queen.

10. lozenge - 1. a figure with four equal sides and two acute and two obtuse angles; diamond; 2. something shaped like a lozenge; specifically: a small, often medicated candy.

11. machine - 1. (a) archaic: a constructed thing whether material or immaterial; (b) conveyance, vehicle; specifically: automobile; (c) archaic: a military engine; (d) any of various apparatus formerly used to produce stage effects; (e-1.) an assemblage of parts that transmit forces, motion, and energy one to another in a predetermined manner; (2) an instrument (as a lever) designed to transmit or modify the application of power, force or motion; 2. (a) a living organism or one of its functional systems; (b) a person or organization that acts for a common end together with the agencies they use; (s) a highly organized political group under the leadership of a boss or small clique; 3. a literary device or contrivance introduced for dramatic effect.

12. manufacture - 1. something made from raw materials; 2. (a) the process of making wares by hand or by machinery especially when carried on systematically with division of labor; (b) a productive industry using mechanical power and machinery; 3. the act or process of producing something.

13. sincere - 1. (a) free of dissimulation: not hypocritical: honest (a -- friend) (-- interest); (b) free from adulteration: pure (-- doctrine) (-- wine); 2. marked by genuineness: real, true (a -- work of art).

14. starve - 1. (a) to perish from lack of food; (b) to

suffer extreme hunger; 2. archaic (a) to die of cold;
(b) to suffer greatly from cold; 3. to suffer or perish
from deprivation.

15. virtue - 1. (a) conformity to a standard of right:  mo-
rality; (b) a particular moral excellence; 2. cap:  an
angel of the fifth highest rank; 3. a beneficial quality
or power of a thing; 4. manly strength or courage:
valor; 5. a commendable quality or trait:  merit;
6. a capacity to act:  potency; 7. chastity, especially
in a woman.

## Exercise 38(11)

Note that the student will not find all of these items
listed under synonomies in any one dictionary.  In addition,
students must follow cross references to locate synonomies
for certain items.

AMBITIOUS, ASPIRING, ENTERPRISING describe one who wishes to
rise above his present position or condition.  The AMBITIOUS
man wishes to attain worldly success, and puts forth effort
to this end:  Ambitious for social position.  The ENTERPRIS-
ING man, interested especially in wealth, is characterized
by energy and daring in undertaking projects.  The ASPIRING
man wishes to rise (mentally or spiritually) to a higher
level or plane, or to attain some end that he feels to be
above his ordinary expectations.

LIKELY, APT, LIABLE are not alike in indicating probability;
though APT is used colloquially, and LIABLE mistakenly, in
this sense.  LIKELY is the only one of these words which
means "probable" or to be expected:  it is likely to rain
today.  Hence APT comes to be associated with LIKELY and to
be used formally as a substitute for it:  he is apt at
drawing, he is apt to do well at drawing.  LIABLE should not
be used to mean "probable."  When used with an infinitive,
it may remind one of LIKELY:  he is liable to be arrested.
But the true meaning, susceptibility to something unpleas-
ant, or exposure to risk, becomes evident when it is used
with a prepositional phrase:  he is liable to arrest, liable
to error.

MUTUAL may be used of an interchange of feeling between
two persons (John and Joe are mutual enemies) or may imply
a sharing jointly with others (the mutual efforts of a
group); COMMON implies a being shared by others or by all
the members of a group (our common interests).

DEFACE, DISFIGURE mean to mar the appearance of. DEFACE implies superficial injuries (as by scratching, scribbling, or the removal of detail); DISFIGURE suggests deeper and more permanent injuries.

DIPLOMATIC, POLITIC, TACTFUL imply ability to avoid offending others or hurting their feelings, especially in situations where this is important. DIPLOMATIC suggests a smoothness and skill in handling others, usually in such a way as to attain one's own ends and yet avoid any unpleasantness or opposition: by diplomatic conduct he avoided antagonizing anyone. POLITIC emphasizes expediency or prudence in looking out for one's own interests, thus knowing how to treat people of different types and on different occasions: a truth which is not politic to insist on. TACTFUL suggests a nice touch in the handling of delicate matters or situations and, unlike the other two, often suggests a sincere desire not to hurt the feelings of others: a tactful wife.

FAMOUS is the general word: a famous lighthouse. CELEBRATED originally referred to something commemorated, but now usually refers to someone or something widely known for conspicuous merit, services, etc.: a celebrated writer, EMINENT implies high standing among one's contemporaries, especially in his own profession or craft: an eminent physician.

HUGE, ENORMOUS, IMMENSE imply great magnitude. HUGE, when used of concrete objects, usually adds the idea of massiveness, bulkiness, or even shapelessness: a huge mass of rock, a huge collection of antiques. ENORMOUS, literally out of the norm, applies to what exceeds in extent, magnitude, or degree, a norm or standard: an enormous iceberg, enormous curiosity. IMMENSE, literally not measureable, is particularly applicable to what is exceedingly great, without reference to a standard: immense buildings. All are used figuratively: a huge success, enormous curiosity, immense joy.

EQUANIMITY implies an inherent evenness of temper or disposition that is not easily disturbed; COMPOSURE implies the disciplining of one's emotions in a trying situation or habitual self-possession in the face of excitement.

RESTIVE describes one who is balky, contrary, fidgety, stubbornly resisting control. A RESTLESS person is uneasy, unable to stop moving or to relax, always seeking activity or change.

RAVENOUS, VORACIOUS suggest a greediness for food and usually intense hunger. RAVENOUS implies extreme hunger, or a famished condition: <u>ravenous wild beasts</u>. VORACIOUS implies the eating of a great deal of food, or the disposition to eat a great deal without reference to the degree of hunger (<u>a voracious small boy incessantly eating</u>) or figuratively (<u>a voracious reader</u>).

## Exercise 38(12)

broadcast or broadcasted, broadcasting

focused or focussed, focusing or focussing

dived or dove, diving

got, getting

lent, lending

shrank or shrunk, shrinking

set, setting

taught, teaching

waked or woke, waking

## Exercise 38(13)

| | |
|---|---|
| alumni | fish or fishes (referring to different species) |
| bears or bear | indexes or indices |
| courts-martial | mesdames |
| crises | strata or stratums |
| daisies | |

## Exercise 38(14)

| | |
|---|---|
| worse, worst | oftener, oftenest |
| worse, worst | redder, reddest |

156

littler or less or lesser,    more shyly, most shyly
   littlest or least
lengthier, lengthiest      better, best

more, most

## Exercise 38(15)

1. Corny - Standard in the sense of "of or producing corn."
   Slang in the sense of "countrified, old-fashioned,
   trite, sentimental." (WNW) Colloquial when applied to
   jazz "written or played with self-conscious emotional-
   ism, lacking sophistication or spontaneity or enthusiasm" (ACD)
2. Cool - Standard in reference to temperature. Colloquial
   in the sense of "without exaggeration:  as he lost a
   cool million on the deal."  Slang in the sense of "very
   good, pleasing, etc.; excellent"
3. Flap - Standard in the sense of a hanging part, the
   movement of such a part, or the noise produced by such
   a part.  Colloquial to toss, fold, shut, etc., smartly,
   roughly, or noisily (ACD).  Slang an occasion of excited
   activity; emergency; crisis
4. Foul-up - [Colloq.], to make a mess of; make disordered
   or confused; entangle or bungle (WNW). To throw into
   disorder or confusion; to blunder (SCD)
5. Goof - Slang
6. Hipster - Slang
7. Jerk - Standard when used as a verb.  Slang in the sense
   of "a person regarded as stupid, dull, eccentric, etc."
8. Kibitzer - Colloquial
9. Moll - Slang in the sense of a gangster's mistress or a
   prostitute
10. Snollygoster - Standard (listed only in W7)
11. Wise-up - Slang
12. Yak - Standard in reference to the animal.  Slang in
    sense of "laugh" and "joke" (listed only in W7)

## Exercise 38(16)

1. billabong - Australia
2. chuckwagon - Western United States
3. coulee - Western North America
4. hoecake - Southern United States
5. laager - South Africa
6. petrol - Britain

7. potlatch - Northern Pacific coast (American Indian)
8. pukka - India
9. sharpie - New England


Exercise 38(17)


1. embarrass
2. en'və.lōp (or än'və.lōp)
3. French précis < Latin praecisus, past participle of
   praecidere to cut off < prae-before + caedere to cut
4. rain, rein
5. diffuse, prolix, wordy, redundant
6. re-dun-dant
7. right, accurate, exact, precise
8. synonym, synonymous, synonymy; valve, vector, verb
   verse, version, versus, vice-, vocative, voice, volt,
   voltage, volume, vow; museum, music, musical, musician;
   Roman Catholic Church
9. Look at the end; Art is long, life is short; From out of
   the depths; Shame be to him who thinks evit of it.
10. 25, 525
11. Bill of exchange
12. 693 miles
13. Charlotte
14. Hebrew
15. since, rinse, wince, quince, prince, evince, convince


(Note that Webster's 7th is the only one of the four standard desk dictionaries which offers a vocabulary of rhymes.)


SECTION 39

VOCABULARY

An objective of a composition course is to assist students to develop a better vocabulary. A certain amount can
be accomplished in this respect by assigned readings and
vocabulary tests relative to what has been read. Another
profitable area in which students can spend time is in the
study and formation of words by means of prefixes and suffixes. Some of the more common prefixes and suffixes are
listed on pp. 302-304 of the text, and exercises are provided which involve work with these various prefixes and suffixes. Exercise 39(8) provides good training in the utilization of synonymies to distinguish between words of similar
meaning.

## Exercise 39(1)

| inaccuracy | nonconformity | immutable |
| unadorned | indistinctive | irrational |
| disagreeable | inexplicable | unworkable |

## Exercise 39(2)

| decentralize | disintegrate | displease |
| undo | demagnetize | disqualify |
| disinherit | dissuade | unravel |

(But note that "dissuade" is defined as "persuade not to do" and that "ravel" can mean both "entangle" and "disentangle.")

## Exercise 39(3)

| advancement | denial | promotion |
| calculation | helplessness | rebellion |
| disappearance | judgment | statesmanship |

## Exercise 39(4)

| adviser(or) | communicator | profiter |
| boaster | disturber | sailor |
| commander | preacher | saver |

## Exercise 39(5)

| beautify | idolize | moralize |
| blacken | liquify | pacify |
| captivate | modernize | victimize |

159

| | | |
|---|---|---|
| humorous | restful (less) | thwarted |
| ironic (ical) | speedy | waspish |
| mulish | talkative | whimsical |

Exercise 39(7)

Only the more common meanings are listed here. Specialized meanings are omitted. The reference is <u>Webster's New World</u>.

1. **compatible** - capable of living together harmoniously or getting along well together; in agreement; congruous

2. **demagogue** - orig.) a leader of the common people; a person who tries to stir up the people by appeals to emotion, prejudice, etc. in order to win them over quickly and so gain power.

3. **intimidate** - to make timid; make afraid; overawe; to force or deter with threats or violence; cow

4. **disparage** - to lower in esteem; discredit; to speak slightingly of; show disrespect for; belittle.

5. **ostentatious** - characterized by or given to ostentation; showy; pretentious.

6. **altruistic** - of or motivated by altruism. altruism-unselfish concern for the welfare of others; selflessness.

7. **taciturn** - almost always silent; not liking to talk; uncommunicative.

8. **malign** - <u>v.t.</u> to speak evil of; defame; slander; traduce.

9. **unscrupulous** - not scrupulous; not restrained by ideas of right and wrong; unprincipled.

10. officious - offering unnecessary and unwanted advice or services; meddlesome.

11. facetious - lightly joking; jocular; jocose, especially at an inappropriate time.

12. incentive - stimulating one to take action, work work harder, etc.; encouraging; motivating. noun - something that stimulates one to take action, work harder, etc.; stimulus, encouragement.

13. ambiguous - having two or more possible meanings; not clear; indefinite; uncertain; vague.

14. pragmatic - having to do with the affairs of a state or community; concerned with actual practice, everyday affairs, etc., not with theory or speculation; practical.

15. estrangement-verb, estrange - to remove, as from usual surroundings or associates; keep apart or away; to turn (a person) from an affectionate or friendly attitude to an indifferent, unfriendly, or hostile one; alienate the affections of.

16. promiscuous- consisting of different elements mixed together or mingled without sorting or discrimination; characterized by a lack of discrimination; specif. - engaging in sexual intercourse indiscriminately or with many persons; without plan or purpose; casual.

17. euphoria - a feeling of vigor, well-being, or high spirits, specif. - psychol. one that is exaggerated and without an obvious cause.

18. corpulent - fat; fleshy; stout; obese.

19. transcend - to go beyond the limits of; overstep; exceed (a story that transcends belief); to be superior to; surpass; excel.

20. pompous - full of pomp; stately; magnificent; characterized by exaggerated stateliness; pretentious, as in speech or manner; self-important.

21.  finite      - having measurable or definable limits;
                   not infinite.


## Exercise 39(8)

     Distinctions in meanings are based on synonyms in
Webster's New World Dictionary, 2nd College Edition.  In
instances where synonyms do not cover all of the given
words, meanings of words not given therein are those
reflected by definitions accompanying the main entry words.

1.  quality, the broadest in scope of these terms, refers
    to a characteristic (physical or nonphysical, indivi-
    dual or typical), that constitutes the basic nature
    of a thing or is one of its distinguishing features
    (the quality of mercy); property applies to any
    quality that belongs to a thing by reason of the
    essential nature of the thing (elasticity is a
    property of rubber); character is the scientific or
    formal term for a distinctive or peculiar quality of
    an individual or of a class, species, etc. (a
    hereditary character); an attribute is a quality
    assigned to a thing, especially one that may reasonably
    be deduced as appropriate to it (omnipotence is an
    attribute of God).

2.  neglect implies a failure to carry out some expected
    or required action, either through carelessness or by
    intention (I neglected to wind the clock); omit, in
    this connection, implies a neglecting through over-
    sight, absorption, etc. (she should not omit to visit
    the Louvre); disregard implies inattention or neglect,
    usually intentional (she always disregards his
    wishes); ignore suggests a deliberate disregarding,
    sometimes through stubborn refusal to face the facts
    (but you ignore the necessity for action); overlook
    suggests a failure to see or to take action, either
    inadvertently or indulgently (I'll overlook your
    errors this time).

3.  costly refers to something that costs much and usually
    implies richness, magnificence, rareness, etc. (costly
    gems): it is often applied to that which it would
    cost much in money or effort to correct or replace
    (a costly error); expensive implies a price in excess
    of an article's worth or of the purchaser's ability
    to pay (an expensive hat); valuable, in this connec-

tion, implies such great value as to bring a high
price (a <u>valuable</u> collection); <u>precious</u> is of great
price or value; <u>priceless</u> is of inestimable value,
beyond price.

4.  <u>calm</u>, basically applied to the weather, suggests a
    total absence of agitation or disturbance (a <u>calm</u>
    sea, mind, answer); <u>tranquil</u> implies a more
    intrinsic or permanent peace and quiet than <u>calm</u>
    (they lead a <u>tranquil</u> life); <u>serene</u> suggests an
    exalted tranquility (he died with a <u>serene</u> smile
    on his lips); <u>placid</u> implies an undisturbed or
    unruffled calm and is sometimes used in jocular
    disparagement to suggest dull equanimity (she's as
    <u>placid</u> as a cow); <u>peaceful</u> suggests a lack of
    turbulence or disorder (a <u>peaceful</u> gathering).

5.  <u>eager</u> implies great enthusiasm, zeal, or sometimes
    impatience, in the desire for or pursuit of something
    (<u>eager</u> to begin work); <u>avid</u> suggests an intense,
    sometimes greedy, desire to enjoy or possess something
    (<u>avid</u> for power); <u>keen</u> implies deep interest and a
    spirited readiness to achieve something (the team
    was <u>keen</u> on winning); <u>anxious</u>, in this connection,
    suggests an eagerness that is accompanied with some
    uneasiness over the outcome (<u>anxious</u> to do his best).

6.  <u>puzzle</u> implies such a baffling quality or such intri-
    cacy, as of a problem, situation, etc., that one has
    great difficulty in understanding or solving it;
    <u>perplex</u>, in addition, implies uncertainty or even
    worry as to what to think, say, or do; <u>bewilder</u>
    implies such utter confusion that the mind is
    staggered beyond the ability to think clearly;
    <u>dumbfound</u> specifically implies as its effect a
    nonplussed or confounded state in which one is
    momentarily struck speechless.

7.  <u>fashion</u> is the prevailing custom in dress, manners,
    speech, etc., of a particular place or time, esp.
    as established by the dominant section of society or
    the leaders in the fields of art, literature, etc.;
    <u>style</u> often a close synonym for fashion, in
    discriminating use suggests a distinctive fashion,
    esp. the way of dressing, living, etc., that
    distinguishes persons with money and taste; <u>vogue</u>
    stresses the general acceptance or great popularity
    of a certain fashion; <u>fad</u> stresses the impulsive

enthusiasm with which a fashion is taken up for a short time; _rage_ and _craze_ both stress an intense, sometimes irrational enthusiasm for a passing fashion.

8. _adjust_ describes the bringing of things into proper relation through the use of skill or judgment (to _adjust_ brakes; to _adjust_ differences); _conform_ means to make the same or similar (to _conform_ one's values to another's); _reconcile_ is to settle (a quarrel, etc.) or compose (a difference, etc.).

9. _correct_ connotes little more than absence of error (a _correct_ answer) or adherence to conventionality (_correct_ behavior); _accurate_ implies a positive exercise of care to obtain conf rmity with fact or truth (an _accurate_ account of the events); _exact_ stresses perfect conformity to fact, truth, or some standard (the _exact_ time, an _exact_ quotation); _precise_ suggests fastidious attitude (_precise_ in all his habits).

10. _hinder_ implies a holding back of something about to begin and connotes a thwarting of progress; _obstruct_ implies a retarding of passage or progress by placing onstacles in the way; _block_ implies the complete, but not necessarily permanent, obstruction of a passage or progress; _impede_ suggests a slowing up of movement or progress by interfering with normal action; _bar_ implies an obstructing as if by means of a barrier; _dam_ means (1) to keep back by means of a dam; hence, (2) to keep back or confine (usually with _in_ or _up_).

11. _ghastly_ suggests the horror aroused by the sight or suggestion of death; _grim_ implies hideously repellent aspects; _grisly_ suggests an appearance that causes one to shudder with horror; _gruesome_ suggests the fear and loathing aroused by something horrible and sinister; _macabre_ implies concern with gruesome aspects of death.

12. _plan_ refers to any detailed method formulated beforehand, for doing or making something; _design_ stresses the final outcome of a plan and implies the use of skill or craft, sometimes in an unfavorable sense, in executing or arranging this; _scheme_, a less definite term than the preceding, often connotes either an impractical, visionary plan

or an underhand intrigue; <u>plot</u> is used of a secret,
usually evil, project or scheme the details of which
have been carefully worked out.

13. <u>copy</u> implies as nearly exact imitation or reproduction
as is possible; <u>mimic</u> suggests close imitation, often
in fun or ridicule; <u>mock</u> implies imitation with the
intent to deride or affront; <u>ape</u> implies close
imitation either in mimicry or in servile emulation.

14. <u>maudlin</u> is that which is tearfully or weakly sentimental in a foolish way (an intoxicated, <u>maudlin</u>
guest); <u>mushy</u> is a colloquial expression meaning
the same as <u>maudlin</u>; <u>sentimental</u> suggests emotion
of a kind that is felt in a nostalgic or tender mood
(<u>sentimental</u> music) or emotion that is exaggerated,
affected, foolish, etc. (a trashy, sentimental novel).

15. <u>malice</u> implies a deep-seated animosity that delights
in causing others to suffer or in seeing them suffer;
<u>spite</u> suggests a mean desire to hurt, annoy, or
frustrate others, usually as displayed in petty,
vindictive acts; <u>grudge</u> implies ill will inspired
by resentment over a grievance.

SECTION 40

EXACTNESS

Since section 40 concerns itself with the exact meanings of words, various exercises are provided to assist student understanding in such matters as confusion of words
with similar sounds or spelling but with different meanings,
improprieties, changes in meaning from one suffixal form of
a word to another, elegant variation, and idiomatic use of
words and phrases. The list of idiomatic prepositions used
after verbs and adjectives on pp. 315-316 of the text may
prove to be particularly helpful to students.

Exercise 40a(1)

1. A garish person is vulgarly showy. Substitute exciting,
   sparkling, brilliant, stirring, etc.
2. Obstinacy is unreasonable inflexibility. Substitute
   fearlessness, firmness, courage, boldness, doggedness,
   etc.
3. Intimidation is obviously a malapropism. Substitute
   indignation.
4. A pretext is a fictitious reason or motive advanced to
   conceal a real one. Substitute reason, justification,
   etc.
5. A pedantic person makes needless display of his learning
   and insists on the importance of trifling points of
   scholarship. Substitute learned.

Exercise 40a(2)

1. Ignorant - implies a lack of knowledge, either generally
   (an ignorant man) or on some particular subject (ignorant of the reason for their quarrel); illiterate
   implies a failure to conform to some standard of knowledge, especially, an inability to read or write; unlettered often implies unfamiliarity with fine literature (although a graduate engineer, he is relatively
   unlettered); uneducated and untutored imply a lack of
   formal systematic education, as of that acquired in
   schools (his brilliant, though uneducated, mind).

2. Detached - implies an impartiality or aloofness resulting from a lack of emotional involvement in a situation
(he viewed the struggle with detached interest);
disinterested strictly implies a commendable impartiality resulting from a lack of selfish motive or desire
for personal gain (a disinterested journalist), but it
is now often used colloquially to mean not interested,
or indifferent; indifferent implies either apathy or
neutrality, especially with reference to choice (to remain indifferent in a dispute); unconcerned implies a
lack of concern, solicitude, or anxiety, as because of
callousness, ingenuousness, etc. (to remain unconcerned
in a time of danger).
3. Excuse - implies a passing over of a fault, omission, or
failure without censure or due punishment in view of
extenuating circumstances; condone suggests an accepting
without protest or censure some reprehensible act or
condition; pardon implies the freeing from the penalty
due for admitted or proved offense; forgive implies the
giving up not only of any claim to requital or retribu-
tion but also of any resentment or desire for revenge.
4. Rebellion - implies open, organized, and often armed
resistance to authority; revolution applies to a
successful rebellion resulting in a change usually in
government; insurrection implies an armed uprising that
quickly fails or succeeds; mutiny applies to group
insubordination or insurrection especially against
maritime or naval authority.
5. Fierce - applies to men and animals that inspire terror
because of their wild and menacing aspect or fury in
attack; ferocious implies extreme fierceness and un-
restrained violence and brutality; barbarous implies a
ferocity or mercilessness regarded as unworthy of
civilized men; savage implies the absence of inhibitions
restraining civilized men filled with rage, lust, or
other violent passion; cruel implies indifference to
suffering and even positive pleasure in inflicting it;
inhuman implies a lack of those characteristics considered normal to human beings.

Exercise 40b (American College)

1. adapt - to make suitable to requirements; adept - one
who has attained proficiency; adopt - to choose for or
take to oneself.
2. alley - a narrow, back street; ally - to unite by
marriage, treaty, league, or confederacy.

3. <u>allude</u> – to make an allusion; <u>elude</u> – to avoid or escape by dexterity or artifice.

4. <u>anecdote</u> – a short narrative of a particular incident or occurrence of an interesting nature; <u>antidote</u> – a medicine or other remedy for counteracting injurious effects.

5. <u>anesthetic</u> – a substance such as ether, chloroform, cocaine, etc., that produces anesthesia; <u>antiseptic</u> – pertaining to or affecting antisepsis.

6. <u>angel</u> – one of a class of spiritual beings, attendants of God; <u>angle</u> – the space within two lines or three planes diverging from a common line.

7. <u>arraign</u> – to call or bring before a court to answer to a charge or accusation; <u>arrange</u> – to place in proper, desired, or convenient order.

8. <u>bloc</u> – a coalition of factions or parties for a particular measure or purpose; <u>block</u> – a solid mass of wood, stone, etc., usually with one or more plane or approximately plane faces.

9. <u>borne</u> – pp. of <u>bear</u> in all meanings except in the sense "brought forth" where <u>born</u> is now used; <u>born</u> – brought forth by birth.

10. <u>Calvary</u> – Golgotha, the place where Jesus was crucified; <u>cavalry</u> – that part of a military force composed of troops that serve on horseback.

11. <u>cannon</u> – a mounted gun for firing heavy projectiles; <u>canon</u> – an ecclesiastical rule or law enacted by a council or other competent authority.

12. <u>canvas</u> – a closely woven, heavy cloth of hemp, flax or cotton, used for tents, sails, etc.; <u>canvass</u> – to examine carefully.

13. <u>carton</u> – a cardboard box; <u>cartoon</u> – a sketch or drawing as in a newspaper or periodical, symbolizing or caricaturing some subject or person of current interest in an exaggerated way.

14. <u>chord</u> – a string of a musical instrument; a combination of three or more tones in harmonic relation; <u>cord</u> – a string or small rope composed of several strands twisted or woven together.

15. <u>climactic</u> – pertaining to or forming a climax; <u>climatic</u> – pertaining to weather conditions of a region.

16. <u>confidently</u> – having strong belief or full assurance; <u>confidentially</u> – spoken or written in confidence.

17. <u>costume</u> – the style of dress, including ornaments and the way of wearing the hair, especially that belonging to a nation, class, or period; <u>custom</u> – a habitual practice.

18. <u>elicit</u> - to draw or bring out or forth; <u>illicit</u> - not permitted or authorized.

19. <u>epic</u> - denoting or pertaining to poetic composition in which a series of heroic achievements or events, usually of a hero, is dealt with at length as a continuous narrative in elevated style; <u>epoch</u> - a particular period of time as marked by distinctive character, events, etc.

20. <u>flaunt</u> - to parade or display oneself conspicuously or boldly; <u>flout</u> - to mock, scoff at, treat with disdain or contempt.

21. <u>genteel</u> - belonging or suited to polite society; <u>gentile</u> - of or pertaining to any people not Jewish.

22. <u>historic</u> - well-known or important in history; <u>historical</u> - relating to or concerned with history or historical events.

23. <u>human</u> - of, pertaining to, or characteristic of man; <u>humane</u> - characterized by tenderness and compassion for the suffering or distressed.

24. <u>ingenious</u> - (of things, actions, etc.) showing cleverness of inventive faculty; <u>ingenuous</u> - free from reserve, restraint, or dissimulation.

25. <u>marital</u> - of or pertaining to marriage; <u>martial</u> - inclined or disposed to war.

26. <u>morality</u> - conformity to the rules of right conduct; <u>mortality</u> - the condition of being mortal or subject to death.

27. <u>prescribe</u> - to lay down in writing or otherwise, as a rule or a course to be followed; <u>proscribe</u> - to denounce or condemn (a thing) as dangerous.

28. <u>receipt</u> - a written acknowledgment of having received money, goods, etc., specified; <u>recipe</u> - any formula, especially one for preparing a dish in cookery.

29. <u>statue</u> - a representation of a person or an animal carved in stone or wood, molded in a plastic material, or cast in bronze or the like; <u>statute</u> - an enactment made by a legislature and expressed in a formal document.

30. <u>waive</u> - to forbear to insist on; <u>wave</u> - a disturbance of the surface of a liquid body, as the sea or a lake, in the form of a ridge or swell.


Exercise 40c

1. irresponsible    2. savagery    3. nonpolitical

4. unpredictable    5. disappearance, silencing

6. Nixon, Truman--or Truman-like   7. schoolteacher

8. peculiar   9. disciplinary   10. liberal

## Exercise 40d

1. irritated   2. imply   3. full of
stop lights

4. inferred   5. ---   6. ---

7. dried him with   8. spend our
a towel   holiday

9. cross the country in our jeep   10. teaching

## Exercise 40e

1. An arguable point is open to dispute or question; an argued point has been or is being disputed or questioned.
2. A practical solution is one that seems to have met the demands of actual living or use; a practicable solution is one that seems feasible but has not been actually tested in use.
3. A hated person is intensely disliked; a hateful person excites or deserves hate.
4. A liberal foreign minister is one who is an advocate of liberalism; a liberated foreign minister is one who has been set at liberty.
5. A single effect is only one effect; a singular effect is an extraordinary or an unusual effect.
6. An intelligible writer is capable of being understood; an intelligent writer is one with good understanding or mental capacity.
7. A godly man is pious; a godlike man is like God or a god.
8. An informed teacher possesses knowledge or information; an informative teacher communicates information.
9. A peaceful nation is free from strife; a peaceable nation is inclined to avoid strife.
10. A workable arrangement is capable of being worked; a working arrangement is one that works.
11. An amicable teacher is friendly, peaceable; an amiable teacher is pleasing in disposition.
12. A yellow piece of paper is of a bright color like that of ripe lemons; a yellowed piece of paper has changed (with age) to a sallow color.

## Exercise 40f(2)

The paragraph uses a number of hackneyed terms as it refers to Marty Jerome: <u>diminutive</u>, <u>pint-sized</u>, <u>little fellow</u>, <u>mighty mite</u>, <u>the tiny Jerome</u>, and <u>little</u> man. In referring to his activities it describes them in such terms as <u>scampered</u>, <u>bulled</u>, <u>hit the ground</u>, <u>85 long and</u> magnificent <u>yards</u>, <u>rabbit-run</u>, <u>bullet-like plunges</u>, <u>like a streak of light</u>, and <u>bulled his way over</u>. In referring to game action such terms are employed as <u>final frame</u>, <u>marker</u>, <u>paydirt</u>, <u>last frame</u>, <u>tallies</u>, and <u>home base</u>.

## Exercise 40g(1)

1. to, with
2. of, from
3. to, with
4. for, into
5. with, to
6. with, to
7. to(with), with
8. from, to(for)
9. to(of), to
10. into, to

## Exercise 40g(2)

1. <u>heedlessly</u>
2. <u>sleeping habits...changed</u>
3. An <u>impression</u> is an effect produced on the intellect, feelings, or conscience: My first impression of the neighbor's dog was that he was hostile. / When I first encountered the neighbor's dog, I left with the impression that...
4. <u>disastrous</u>
5. <u>confident</u>
6. <u>imbued</u>
7. <u>displayed</u>
8. <u>moved</u>
9. To commiserate is to condole or sympathise with. It is doubtful if any judge would have such feelings for those committing such a heinous act. The phrase "had nothing but contempt," however, might be a more accurate reflection of the judge's feelings.
10. <u>suspect</u> not <u>skeptical</u>

1. uttered, whispered, murmured, shouted, roared, exclaimed, whined, grumbled, soliloquized, declaimed, spouted, ranted, recited, lectured, sermonized, expatiated
2. scribbled, scrawled, inscribed, copied, engraved, transcribed, recorded, typewrote
3. strike, knock, rap, slap, thump, beat, bong, slam, punch, pelt, kick, butt, pat
4. sobbed, wept, moaned, whined, whimpered, wailed, puled, lamented, screamed, shrieked
5. formed, constructed, manufactured, erected, established, organized, produced, structured, invented, founded
6. preceded, outranked, headed, conducted, guided, escorted, commanded, excelled
7. devour, swallow, gulp, bolt, bite, munch, crunch, chew, nibble, gnaw, sup, gorge, stuff, gormandize, taste, savor
8. improve, mend, ameliorate, repair, remedy, prune, revise, edit, redact, reform, palliate, refine, rectify, amend, chasten, discipline
9. bruise, pound, crush, burst, crack, split, tear, rend, fracture, shatter, smash, disjoin, disconnect, dissociate, detach, sunder, divide, mangle, dissect, disintegrate
10. hasten, scurry, scamper, race, fly, rush, dash, trot, gallop, flit, spring, dart, whiz

## DIRECTNESS

Directness of expression gives many students trouble. Oftentimes, one of the most difficult points to get across to students is that the clearest writing and the best writing is that which is the simplest and the most direct. Too often, students are inclined to confuse pomposity and wordiness with intellectuality. Prying them away from such propensities is like taking candy from a baby; in either instance, to pursue the comparison to its ultimate, unless matters are corrected, the results can become rather messy. To assist in this area, section 41 of the text provides discussions and exercises relative to deadwood; circumlocutions; awkward repetition; and simple, direct expressions. Exercises 41 and 41a-e provide good tests of student understanding in the area of direct expression.

### Exercise 41a

1. The fastest automobile requires the best gasoline.
2. Mr. Armstrong, my history teacher, has an interesting classroom manner.
3. I have two reasons for not going: First, I have to study for an examination; second, I have no money.
4. Jim jogged every morning because he believed exercise was healthful.
5. Dr. Mackenzie is one of the most interesting lecturers I have ever heard.
6. Love and understanding are two of the most important things young children need.
7. This book covers the basic fundamentals of good English.
8. Most congressmen spend most of each working day attending subcommittee meetings.
9. After spending several hours shopping for mother's gift, I finally decided to give her a check to buy whatever she might prefer.
10. After he finished his navy service, he decided to enroll again in school.

### Exercise 41b

actual - real and true

literature - plays and poems

environment - life and times

esteem - love and regard

precious - costly and dear

astounded - amazed and surprised

stern - severe and strict

level - flat and even

arrogant - proud and vain

scrupulous - conscientious and honest

## Exercise 41c

1. It was the consensus among the students that grades should be abandoned.
2. Teachers should provide several illustrations of the grammatical rules they are trying to teach.
3. I would classify Joyce as a very difficult author to read.
4. The Administration hasn't lowered the taxes it has countless times promised to reduce.
5. Today's student wants primarily to apply in life what he has learned.
6. I like rock and roll as well as the next person, but it becomes boring after I have listened to it for a whole afternoon.
7. The good writer is always sincere.
8. The instructor said firmly that the class would meet at 9:00 A.M.
9. We had planned to return to the house before nightfall.
10. The car sped down the highway for several miles before it skidded out of control.

## Exercise 41d

1. The instructor assigned Tom Jones, but most of the students read digests of the novel.
2. Always check the location of the fire escape so you can escape if there is a fire.

3. Instead of working he was recounting what had happened to him on the way to the office.
4. He is an industrial engineering student concerned with the principles of time and motion.
5. In my opinion, government should not intervene in private business.
6. A reckless driver is no better than a murderer.
7. A student should investigate different fields before deciding what he wants to major in.
8. As the band struck up "Hail to the Chief," the President and the First Lady descended the staircase.
9. Not long ago, it was difficult for people to believe that a spaceship could land on the moon.
10. Last night we had to circle the block before finding a parking space.

## Exercise 41a-e

1. The United States cannot expect to spread peace to other countries until we teach our own people to respect each other.
2. He is capable of working long hours each day.
3. The integration of public schools is a major step toward equality.
4. During his whole college career, Peter planned to work his way around the world.
5. Only in the past couple of years have black Americans begun to make it clear that they wish to develop their own racial identity.
6. Nixon chose Agnew as a running-mate for Vice-President because he wanted a Southern candidate as a nominee.
7. The first settlers in the West explored as they prospected for gold.
8. The actress performed very badly, but the play continued to its end.
9. He was the handsomest man I had ever seen.
10. Pollution in our waterways has troubled scientists for one and a half decades.

APPROPRIATENESS

Although instructors may vary somewhat in the level of writing that they will accept from their students, few will accept anything less than an informal level. The difference, of course, between formal, informal, and substandard levels is not always readily perceivable to the student. For this reason, section 42 comprises discussion and exercises relative to such aspects of usage as slang, substandard English, trite expressions, jargon, stilted diction, and mixed and incongruous metaphors. Sometimes, of course, what is suitable for one audience will not be suitable for another. Exercise 42a-f provides for consideration as to whether or not the diction employed in some sample writing is suitable for certain types of audiences. The "Diction" Review Exercise on p. 336 provides a good test regarding the elements of exactness, directness, and appropriateness in writing.


Exercise 42c(1)

wily Indians; to strike while the iron was hot; the break of dawn; The hardy pioneers; in unison; veritable hail of bullets; the pesky redskins keeled over and bit the dust; The rugged frontiersmen; to give a good account of themselves; broad daylight; broke through the ramparts; their backs against the wall; slaughtered mercilessly; When the dust had risen from the battlefield; when the smoke had cleared away; carnage was frightful; Every single; gone to meet his maker.


Exercise 42c(2)

The American Way ... feasible route ... to tread; educational personnel; educational institutions of learning; humble origins; child of adversity; born in a log cabin; beyond a shadow of a doubt; reached the summits; fair country of ours; There is too much of a tendency to view ... with alarm; great institution; But on the other hand; people who live in glass houses; the type most inclined to cast aspersions; wet blankets; the ones by whom criticisms are

made; Now I'm just ... should be run; Abe Lincoln, if he
were alive; newfangled techniques; making a shambles of; at
the bottom of; our American heritage; the American Way;
notorious radicals; wreaked havoc with our boys and girls.

## Exercise 42f

1. He encountered a disastrous eddy as he swam through
   the sea of life.
2. Jim brought his big guns to the debate and shot down
   his opponent.
3. The flowers on the table imparted a pleasant aroma
   to the atmosphere.
4. The young teacher is rapidly gaining stature in the
   eyes of the student.
5. We're skating on thin ice and if it breaks we'll
   enjoy a cold water bath.
6. The Senate wanted to plug the loopholes in the tax
   bill but it couldn't because too many important
   people were interested in keeping them open.
7. He worked as busily as a beaver, but one day he
   became so ill that he decided to do a little less
   dam building in the future.
8. My constantly misplacing my glasses makes me blind,
   although I know my apartment as a bat knows his cave.
9. Although she was head over heels in love with him,
   she still managed a level head about the matter.
10. He had his back to the wall; then he had his
    inspiration and he was able to move forward.

## "Diction" Review Exercise

### (Sections 40 through 42)

1. He was trying to keep abreast of company developments;
   but because he kept getting behind, his reputation
   ebbed.
2. A college student has to study a lot if he is going
   to be a successful student.
3. C. B. Brown must have worked very hard to complete
   six Gothic novels in less than four years.
4. Many beginning Bilingual Education instructors are
   weak in instructional methodology.
5. Indications are that one Joshua Fiddings wrote the
   novel.
6. The campus police theorized that the burglars entered
   through the cafe.

177

7. My little sister's pretty face becomes very red when my brother beats her unmercifully in ping-pong.
8. Mr. Smith was the bane of his wife's existence because he frequently forgot her shopping instructions.
9. We want you to feel free to ask for anything you need to make you comfortable.
10. Professor Caitlin was poor financially, but he was so well regarded that more students in the college remembered him than any other teacher.
11. Coaches are paid for teams that win games.
12. I was filled with anger when my expensive stereo equipment was destroyed by the vandals. (rage, precious, and ruined can be substituted for anger, expensive and destroyed).
13. I thought I was doing the best thing when I enlisted in the army.
14. Even though homemaking is an important occupation, only a few homemakers have been thoroughly prepared for the task.
15. By reading Yachting, I am able to keep informed about sailing activities.


SECTION 43

GLOSSARY OF USAGE

The Glossary of Usage which is set forth in section 43 provides a very helpful guide to the student of the usage levels of various words and expressions. Although most instructors will probably not want to spend a great deal of time on this section, many will want to take steps to insure that students have familiarized themselves with it because it does provide a good alphabetical reference guide that students should utilize when they are in doubt about the acceptability of certain expressions.

SPELLING

Spelling is one of the most troublesome areas for many
college students, and what to do about it can be a matter of
considerable perplexity to the instructor.  College seems to
be a rather late stage for the learning of proper spelling;
on the other hand, if college students cannot spell well,
the instructor can scarcely avoid the luxury of ignoring the
situation.  At the same time, a composition course is not a
spelling course; therefore the instructor must decide how he
can do the most about spelling deficiencies in the limited
time that can reasonably be devoted to the matter.  Section
44 includes a discussion of certain aspects of spelling that
can be studied with benefit to some students.  Many of the
rules of spelling are given, and lists of some of the most
commonly mispronounced words and most frequently misspelled
words are included.  Requiring students to be able to spell
the words in these lists will not enable them to correct all
of the spelling errors they will make, but since the words
are among those which are most commonly misspelled, if students can learn to spell these words it should assist them
to avoid making many of the spelling errors they might otherwise make.

The instructor may also desire to emphasize the spelling of certain words which are pronounced the same or about
the same (e.g. their, they're, there; too, two, to; and its,
it's).  Actually, such words bring out a very important fact
that many instructors will want to stress.  This is that
what is really involved in such instances is not misspelling
at all but rather a misunderstanding of the words function-
ally.  In other words, students can be helped to avoid
misspelling the variant forms their, they're and there by
being made to understand that their is the possessive of they
and hence is an adjective; there, by comparison, is usually
an adverb indicating place; and they're is a contraction for
they are.  Similarly too is an adverb denoting intensifica-
tion with regard to a word modified; to is either a preposition, or part of an infinitive; two of course indicates a
number.  By the same token, its and it's often give a great
deal of trouble which can be avoided once it is understood
that it is one of the few words whose possessive form is
indicated without the use of the apostrophe and that it's is

never possessive, but a contraction of <u>it is</u>.

## Exercise 44e(1)

Rule notations are with respect to paragraphs wherein rule is discussed in text.

argument - exception to rule 2b

beggar - rule 4

buried - rule 3

conceivable - rule 2a

eightieth - rule 3

association - rule 2a

hoping - rule 2

drooping - rule 4

changeable - exception to rule 2a

changing - rule 2

awful - exception to rule 2b

precedence - rule 2

shining - rule 2

business - rule 3

deferred - rule 4

peaceable - exception to rule 2a

## Exercise 44e(2)

Rule notations are with respect to paragraphs wherein rule is discussed in text.

| | | | |
|---|---|---|---|
| 1. | frames, rule 5 | 11. | echoes, rule 6 |
| 2. | roses, rule 5 | 12. | strata, rule 9 |
| 3. | dashes, rule 6 | 13. | churches, rule 6 |
| 4. | mazes, rule 5 | 14. | ladies, rule 7 |
| 5. | tables, rule 5 | 15. | masses, rule 6 |
| 6. | branches, rule 6 | 16. | Charleses, rule 6 |
| 7. | basses, rule 6 | 17. | noes, rule 6 |
| 8. | cameos, rule 5 | 18. | potatoes, rule 6 |
| 9. | flies, rule 7 | 19. | plays, rule 8 |
| 10. | boxes, rule 6 | 20. | pains, rule 5 |

## THE LIBRARY AND THE RESEARCH PAPER

Like the dictionary, the library can be of tremendous assistance to a student. One of the most effective methods to insure that he learns how to use it is to require him to go to the library and to familiarize himself with the library catalogs, reference books, the range of books in general, and the various periodicals, bulletins, and pamphlets which the library stocks. Once he has a general knowledge of what is available, the important skill he needs to master is to locate material concerning the topic he is interested in.

Section 45 contains a list of some of the most important reference books including, first of all, guides to reference books, general encyclopedias, dictionaries, word books, year books, atlases and gazeteers, general biographies, and books of quotations. Also listed are reference books relating to mythology and folklore, modern literature, history, music and painting, philosophy and religion, science and technology, and social sciences. Indexes to periodicals, bulletins, and pamphlets are also listed, including not only the widely used Reader's Guide to Periodical Literature and Index to the Social Sciences and Humanities, but many special indexes, some of which relate to specific disciplines.

Section 46 provides for a systematic approach to the matter of writing a research paper, beginning with a discussion of how to choose and limit a subject, and ending with the presentation and discussion of a specimen research paper. A number of sample bibliographical and footnote entries are given--enough to satisfy questions concerning the vast majority of situations involving types of entries with which students will be confronted. The specimen research paper is very thoroughly discussed and comments on a paragraph by paragraph basis concerning the composition of the paper and the manner in which footnoted entries have been made and the way in which they have been cited. A careful study of this sample research paper should be of considerable assistance to students seeking answers to the whys and wherefores of constructing a research paper.

## SECTION 45

## THE LIBRARY

Section 45 provides discussion relative to such important library aspects as the library catalogs, the catalog cards, and library holdings in general. Three very practical exercises are provided which will require the student to investigate the library and utilize some of its resources.

Exercise 45(1) requires the student to go to the library and to indicate on a diagram the locations of twenty five of the most widely used reference books and indexes. Some instructors have found it desirable to prepare a diagram of the library's reference room on a handout sheet on which the student is asked to insert the numbers of the various works involved. This device saves the student time and makes it possible to assign additional work in the library in lieu of the time spent in drawing the diagram.

Exercise 45(2) requires the student to answer various questions by consulting reference books in the library. A good idea when assigning this exercise is to require the students to prepare their answers in complete sentences and to italicize the work from which they elicited their reply. Such a requirement achieves training in writing good sentences and italicizing book and periodical titles.

Exercise 45(3) is a meaningful assignment that requires students to examine certain works in some detail and to summarize properly the information such works contain. A start in proper documentation can be made with this exercise by requiring students to quote material taken from these works in the preparation of the exercise.

### Exercise 45(2)

1. The Jewish Encyclopedia, 8, pp. 493-495
2. Tlingit tribe. Encyclopedia of Religion and Ethics, XI, 443.
3. For two partners: 1 rocker; 1 dipper; 2 buckets (to carry the dirt in); 2 shovels; 1 pick; 1 pan. Encyclopedia Americana, XI, 524b.
4. In 12th-century England, gossip meant "a godparent." (Oxford English Dictionary).

5. Five. <u>Education Index</u>, XI, 898. (Twelve articles are listed for period June 1957-June 1959.)
6. <u>International Index</u>, XIV and XV.
7. <u>Agricultural Index</u> and <u>Industrial Arts Index</u>.
8. <u>Art Index</u>, X and XI ("Glass painting and staining, French").
9. Washing machine. <u>Dictionary of American Biography</u>, V, 410.
10. <u>Dictionary of National Biography</u>, 16, p. 788.
11. $5.19 (Publishers Library Binding), Pantheon.
12. 1021. <u>Statistical Abstract of The United States</u>, 1971, p. 568.

## THE RESEARCH PAPER

Instructor attitudes toward the research paper vary quite widely at the present. There appears to be more and more of a trend toward the writing of a short documented paper of 1000-1500 words in lieu of the longer research paper that has often been favored in the past. The reasoning behind this change in point of view takes into consideration many factors. One is the regrettable tendency on the part of many students to copy excerpts from many different sources into one synthesized whole and to present the final effort as an original one. Unfortunately, even though the ends of research may have been somewhat served by such activity, the more important aspect of dealing with the research paper in an honest, professional manner has not. Of course, writing a shorter paper will not in itself result in an absence of plagiarism, inadvertent or otherwise, but the mere fact that the writing assignment is of relatively short length and hence will involve fewer research sources tends to put the emphasis on documentation and proper summarization rather than on a frenzied gathering of material from diverse sources. As a further end to proper documentation and summarization, many instructors prefer to use a good case book. A case book involves the disadvantage of lack of original research; however, many will contend that first things come first and, hence, learning how to properly extract and report from other sources is the skill that is most important in the initial stages of the student's research writing career. In other words, learning how to handle properly the research material must occur before any accurate, meaningful account of research activities can take place.

Section 46 discusses the choosing and limiting of a research paper topic, and Exercise 46(1) presents a list of questions. As students obtain the answers to these questions, they should be provided with the idea for a good research paper subject. The technique of asking questions about a prospective subject area is good in that it helps provide the student some initial positive direction. If a particular question intrigues him, he may become quite interested in getting the answer to that question. This is the very essence of constructive research endeavor--to find out something about a subject that one wishes to know about.

A number of good specimen bibliography cards and exercises relating to the handling of bibliographical entries are supplied. Exercises 46(3) and 46(4) provide good practical working experience for the student in preparing bibliographical cards and preparing short working bibliographies.

At the time they are dealing with the note-taking aspect of the research paper, many instructors will want to assign work involving summarization which may involve several of the exercises in section 47. Effective summarization and quotation is perhaps, more than anything else, the most important and the most difficult phase of the research paper. Much of the plagiarism that occurs in the research paper is inadvertent and results not from deliberate dishonesty on the part of the student but from a lack of the ability to present in his own words what it is that someone else has said. Developing student ability to summarize accurately and skillfully is a monumentally difficult task, and positive results in this respect will not be easy to come by. Any degree of success in this respect, consequently, will usually be achieved only as the result of sustained and repetitive endeavor.

Several aspects of note-taking can be emphasized which will assist in the proper utilization of note cards. First of all, the students can be made to understand that note cards can be of three types:
(1) the note card which involves the copying of material from another source. One very important point to emphasize in this connection is that whenever material is taken from another source, it must be included in quotation marks. Such a procedure will insure that when the student uses the material on the card he will recognize that the words are those of another, and he will give proper credit to the reference source when he incorporates the material into his paper.
(2) the note card which contains the student's summarization of what another source says. An excellent admonition to stress relative to this type of note card is that as the student summarizes, he should do so without direct reference to the source material. In short, if a student can be trained to write his summarizations by closing the reference source before he prepares his account, what will result will be in his own words and not those of the original author.

(3) <u>the note card which contains only words and phrases involving another source.</u> This is often a good type of note card to emphasize, since it requires the student to elaborate in his own words upon ideas or comments of others, or upon factual material as the case may be.

The requirement that all three of these types of note cards be used should result in a research paper which strikes a happy balance between quotations and summarizations--one which will avoid plagiarism.

The question of how to handle footnote cards can be a vexing one to the instructor. In particular, the reconciliation of footnote entries to the cards can be a very arduous and time consuming task for the instructor. One very effective and timesaving procedure that can be utilized in this connection is the following. This is to require the student to insert blank sheets of paper between the successive typed pages of his paper and then to staple the footnote cards which pertain to footnotes on a particular page on the reverse side of the blank sheet which precedes that page. If he is further required to key the footnote card according to the superscript, a very systematic basis for review is provided for the instructor. After all, what the instructor is primarily interested in is how the footnote cards were used in developing the text of the paper, not the number of cards as such. Therefore, if he has available to him as he reviews the paper the footnote cards upon which the footnotes are based, he can, as he evaluates the paper, quickly determine the effectiveness of the utilization of footnote material by comparing what is on the footnote card on the left page with what is in the term paper page on the right.

A quick visualization as to how such a system works can be obtained by referring to pp. 418-419 of the text. If the footnote card which has been reproduced on p. 418 is imagined as being on a blank sheet of paper and keyed with a "1" to indicate that it applies to footnote 1 on the right-hand side, the ease with which the footnote card can be compared to the text should be readily apparent. In the event the same footnote card is used for more than one footnote, the subsequent reference can be handled by another footnote card which will refer to the previous footnote card with the brief note "See footnote card #1," or, of course, whatever previous footnote card is involved.

A number of good specimen footnotes are included in the text. These samples should provide adequate assistance in the vast majority of footnote entries that the student will be concerned with. A discussion is also provided on pp. 411-413 as to how to introduce quoted material. Since many students tend to overuse quoted material, many instructors will want to emphasize very strongly that research papers should include only a few quotations and that when they are used, the mechanics of proper quotation must be scrupulously observed.

It may be quite profitable to spend considerable time in class in going over the specimen research paper on pp. 415-442 of the text. The text authors have provided many penetrating comments on the pages preceding the specimen pages of the sample research paper as to why the research paper writer has prepared the paper in the way that he has. Instructors may wish to discuss several of these points to insure that the students thoroughly understand the methods which have been employed in writing the paper.

SECTION 47

WRITING SUMMARIES

Section 47 is a short section of the Prentice-Hall Handbook for Writers, but the fact that the section is short should not obscure the fact that the section is a very important one. As has already been commented in the remarks relative to section 46, the student's ability to put into his own words what others have said is all important in the proper development of a research paper. Unfortunately, a great number of students cannot do this and will be unable to do it without a great deal of practice.

Section 47 contains a good discussion as to how to approach the problem of summarization, stressing first of all that the student should attempt to determine the author's purpose and his point of view. If the student can do this--in effect, what he is doing in this connection is eliciting the main idea of the paragraph or the work under consideration--he is proving his ability to get quickly to the core of the material. If such is accomplished, he has certainly developed an ability which will stand him in very good stead not only in his summarization of material for

research paper purposes, but also in his reading relative
to many other courses.

Exercises 47(1)-47(4) require the student to construct
sentence precis relative to various paragraphs. All provide
good training in eliciting the main ideas of paragraphs and
presenting such ideas in condensed, precise prose. Instructors who desire to provide additional summarization training
for students may desire to utilize others of the paragraphs
contained on pp. 227-233 of the text in addition to the one
suggested by exercise 47(1), which involves an excerpt from
Jacques Barzun's Teacher in America.

A variation in the writing of summaries which may be
particularly helpful can be achieved by requiring students
to write two different summary versions of a paragraph, one
of which involves a quotation or two from the paragraph, and
another which does not. Still another summarization technique which students need training in is one involving a
situation in which it is necessary to quote one writer who
is quoting another (this may often involve a quotation
within a quotation). In this connection, a good summarization exercise can be to require the students to prepare a
summary, say of the first paragraph of the sample research
paper on p. 421 of the text in which they can be required to
deal with the remarks of Dr. Harden as they are quoted in
Mr. O'Hare's paper. Other paragraphs in the sample research
paper can be used for the same purpose.

### Exercise 47(1)

The purpose of good teaching is to train youngsters
not only to learn but to study on their own. Training students to think is more important than requiring them to
memorize things.

### Exercise 47(2)

The purpose of good teaching is to train students to
work things out for themselves rather than to memorize.

### Exercise 47(3)

Students who participate in dietary training benefit
because they learn about people from other sections, they

mature, and they become more independent and self-sufficient.

## Exercise 47(4)

Nothing, neither torrents of rain nor endless portraits of Stalin, can dampen the enthusiasm of Russians for their pageants and popular feasts; and they insist that their foreign guests enjoy the pretty girls, the flowers, the floats, the dancing and singing and marching as much as, and as late as, they do.

## SECTION 49

### AN INDEX TO GRAMMATICAL TERMS

Section 49 is probably not a section that many instructors would want to assign for class discussion since it is, in effect, a capsule explanation of various terms which are treated more fully in other parts of the textbook. It is nonetheless a section which can be very valuable for quick reference purposes, and many instructors will want to familiarize themselves with it to be able to direct students to it when the latter are having trouble discussing or understanding some particular aspect of grammar. This section can also be commended to students as providing a quick overall review of the grammar section of the handbook. As such it can help the student determine for himself the extent to which he understands the various grammatical terms and perhaps serve as a motivation for review of certain aspects which he still does not understand too well.